# THE DAY THE SKY BROKE OPEN

# *The Day the Sky Broke Open*

A Memoir

by

**KEITH T. HOERNER**

Adelaide Books
New York / Lisbon
2021

THE DAY THE SKY BROKE OPEN
A Memoir
By Keith T. Hoerner

Copyright © by Keith T. Hoerner
Cover Design © 2021 Adelaide Books
Cover Photo by Zoltan Tasi via Unsplash

Published by Adelaide Books, New York / Lisbon
adelaidebooks.org

Editor-in-Chief
Stevan V. Nikolic

All rights reserved. No part of this book may be reproduced in any manner whatsoever without written permission from the author except in the case of brief quotations embodied in critical articles and reviews.

For any information, please address Adelaide Books
at info@adelaidebooks.org
or write to:
Adelaide Books
244 Fifth Ave. Suite D27
New York, NY 10001

ISBN: 978-1-955196-17-8

Printed in the United States of America

PARTIAL PROCEEDS BENEFIT CHILD-ABUSE CHARITIES

*Dedicated to those who suffer(ed) child abuse;*

*my Star People, especially Anne;*

*Arthur W. Frank;*

*John Kotre;*

*Dr. James Pennebaker;*

*Alcoholics Anonymous;*

*and, of course, my Higher Power*

# Contents

*From the Author* **9**

GATHERING STORM / Prologue **13**

RAIN **21**

SKY BREAK **125**

*Epilogue* **149**

*About the Author* **161**

# *From the Author*

The movement in *The Day the Sky Broke Open* is a series of vignettes or jump cuts, similar to modern cinematic technique, exemplifying the fact that chaotic stories often have an absence of smooth transition and order.

Drawing from the text *The Wounded Storyteller*, this creative nonfiction witness recounts a dysfunctional upbringing within the structure of what Arthur W. Frank purports as The Chaos Narrative. I write this piece to reclaim myself, to find my voice from beneath an antagonist who made me mute. Surprisingly, in reshaping the fractured pieces of my so-called life, I also discovered the existence of varied selves along the way (not only the ever-present lover but the admitted hater), which I have too long denied.

After nearly 60 years, I am now able to recognize that love and hate can coexist as counter selves in the human heart.

*"If you ever write a story about our family, just make sure I'm dead."*

— Mom

# GATHERING STORM

## *Prologue*

*My mother pierced me in the heart with an arrow when I was 10 years old. I knew it wasn't Cupid's loving projectile – when at 12, her palm on the end of the nock, fingertips pinched around the feathers of the fletching – she pummeled it through me with one blunt thrust. The pain was unexpected, excruciating, numbing.*

*Ironically, my love for Mom was such that I knelt before her: willing to wrap my own hands around the arrow's shaft and thrust it through my chest. I would gladly have offered my life to her; she was my mother. But her plan for me, conscious or otherwise, was something altogether different.*

*I strangely lived with this protrusion stumped from my nearly arrested heart and out my back, until the age of 44. When, working a 12-step recovery program for alcoholism, I slowly, very slowly and with great care, became able to remove the point – so dangerously close to taking not just my physical self but my soul.*

*Now, I am left to tend the wound.*

In telling my story, you are asked not only to read but to listen. Remember, please, to *listen*. For tales such as mine are told "from the edges of a wound… on the edges of speech… [The] chaos is… in the silences that speech cannot penetrate or illuminate" (Frank 101). Metaphors, like the "arrow" previously mentioned, are my attempt to assist where words fail me. They are the crutch upon which my bruised emotional being leans for understanding.

Through Anne, my wife, I was blessed to have been given a divining rod to further seek out the illusive, restorative waters of healing in Arthur W. Frank's text *The Wounded Storyteller*. It has led me to find my voice and reclaim myself from beneath an antagonist who made me mute. This text espouses why:

…ill[ness or physical and mental trauma] is a call for stories… to repair the damage that illness has done to the ill person's sense of where she [or he] is in life, and where she [or he] may be going. Stories [Frank asserts] are a way of redrawing maps and finding new directions.

…These stories are told in conditions of fatigue, uncertainty, sometimes pain, and always fear that turn the ill person into what Ronald Dworkin describes as a "narrative wreck," a phrase displaying equal wit and empathy. (qtd. in Frank 54)

…The way out of the narrative wreckage is telling stories, specifically… "self stories." The self story is not told for the sake of description, though description may be its ostensible content. The self is being *formed* in what is told.

…The self story is told both to others and to one's self; each telling is enfolded within the other. The act of telling is a dual reaffirmation. Relationships with others are reaffirmed, and the self is reaffirmed… The ill person must reaffirm… he [or she] is still there, as an audience [to oneself]. (Frank 53-56)

I reflect on desperately working the coordinates of a new map to a healthier destination. The compass I hold spins wildly.

Having grown-up under the dictate we must never "air our dirty laundry," I would question my intent in writing this account of my dysfunctional childhood. Is it to be vengeful? No, that is not in my making. I simply seek to be reaffirmed. I need to know my essence is viable, the degrading and emasculating indoctrination I lived under was false, the actions taken against me as a child were wrong. Pragmatically, I recognize this; emotionally and in my subconscious, I have fallen ill, and they tell me otherwise.

Sharing my story from the periphery of the wound, memories, as always, are called into question.

My first memory is one of my twin, Kenny, and me as infants. It is 1963, and my mind imagines a jumping film reel, hears the faint klickity klack of an old-time projector. We are finger painting on the wall behind our shared baby bed. But it is not paint. It is blood. And it is a deep charcoal gray, because the film in my head is black and white.

A broken baby bottle lies in the corner, glass remnants trapped between the bed frame and bunting. I have small cuts on my fingers, and their tips need no dipping. They flow as I create.

Kenny reaches up and points to my abstract painting, perhaps an ode to my future or an omen of things to come. He moves his sticky hands to my cheeks, my chest, my toes. We giggle.

This is an odd memory contrasting blood and laughter. It has, of course, been infused with personal inclinations of odes and omens, a film projector, black and white film. I know of no pictures or reels to have been taken of this event. Pragmatically, in fact, I know the standard reaction would be to simply seek-out injury, clean, and bandage. Which I am told did happen. Small cuts were found on our fingers, and no serious attention was needed.

Still, why the out-of-body observing? The projector? The ode/omen? And how could I possibly have a memory from as far back as when I was 10- to 14-months old?

John Kotre, in his text *White Gloves: How We Create Ourselves Through Memory,* answers this by addressing the typical content of first memories:

...studies that covered individuals ranging in age from the teens to the 80s found that most fall into the categories of trauma (a childhood accident, for example)... A number of investigators report that early memories are predominantly visual, and several indicate that such memories are more likely than others to be seen from a vantage point outside the body... It simply seems to be a matter of how old the memory is. The majority of our autobiographical memories never shift into the out-of-body perspective, but those that do are likely to be among our earliest. (194)

I ponder Kortre's assertion that memories of this type are generally traumatic. I recall no pain but a sense of glee as Kenny and I (more me than he – as it is still my nature) happily painted: rubbing, smooshing, trailing our plasma across the clean canvas of a wall, the bed spindles, our blankets, and selves.

The only possibility for trauma comes from a deductive reasoning based on my experience later in life. My sister Kathleen would have been about 11 years old then, approximately the same age as me when I was given the responsibility to parent my brothers, Pete and Brad. My theory is we were startled out of our innocent playfulness into some kind of abstract terror: when upon discovery, my mother attacked Kathleen, whose responsibility she deemed it was to watch over and rear us.

Recall tells me this "jump cut" from happiness to horror was the newly discovered baseline for the chaos I was to live throughout my childhood.

My next memory is sitting in first grade, frightened and insecure, having been kept out of kindergarten to do chores around the house.

I did not recognize at that time my abuse cycle, like a functioning machine, was already well oiled. I was highly passive, eager to please, and lacked self confidence… for the mind control through fear was "jump started" that day in the crib when it was imbedded (a shard of glass from the broken milk bottle) deep in the psyche of my mind.

The ensuing witness of my sister Kathleen (who I considered my mother) being beaten frequently before me accelerated everything. I held hatred against my real mother, I now realize – as far back as then, yet sought her love on what could only be an unhealthy level. I felt if I could prove myself worthy, draw out her love, a miracle might "put to bed" the bedlam Kathleen, and in turn, I would barely breathe through.

Where, too, was my father in all this? I can now ask. Or demand. His patriarchic responsibility was given little accountability in regard to protection. He filed in line with the rest of us.

I seek not to place blame, but the fingers of memory point clearly in these two directions. There was no nurturance. There was no protection. Despite it, I grew relatively strong along a thorny vine with so little water – blooming healthy was but a beautiful dream.

I recall the day when I was 36 years old, and my sister Beth had driven Mom from Kansas City, Missouri, proper, to see Anne's and my new house in Liberty, MO. She had nothing to say other than how nice the exposed aggregate looked. *How weird*, I thought. *What about the 2,600 square feet backing to woods? The hardwood? The acre of land? One comment – and it's about the damn concrete!* God, she exasperated me. She would give me no satisfaction in my success. Though edging toward her 70s, wisdom had not replaced her jealousy.

While Anne showed Beth the house, Mom and I sat at the breakfast-room table, uncommunicative as ever. I looked tiredly at her, thinking of the second DWI charge I had just gotten, then flat out told Mom I believed I was an alcoholic. Her emerald-green eyes glinted, my statement firing her synapses, only to be quickly snuffed, signaling the need for a cigarette to calm her thoughts. Lighting up (regardless of my saying we did not allow smoking in the house), she said, "No, you're *not* an *alcoholic*; you just need to find a bar closer to home."

I now hear the absurdity of her answer. Though then, it gave me the back-up I needed to carry on with my denial (her denial). By merely questioning my impropriety regarding alcohol, I had unwittingly and momentarily begun to survey the damage done, dallying on Arthur W. Frank's course of salvaging the wreckage of my life. The boat looked sturdy stem to stern. But hidden beneath the water, the bow was rotting. Sinking was just a matter of time.

Yet upon Mom's "rechristening," I found the bar closer to home, continued drinking, and collected an unimaginable two more DWI charges – for a total of four: one every three years over 12. By the grace of God, I hurt no one on the road, but I knew – this, too – was just a matter of time. Plea bargaining kept me out of prison. And six years after speaking to Mom about my suspected disease, I "stood at the turning point" as stated in the "Big Book" of *Alcoholics Anonymous* (59).

For me, it was 1) find myself on the path to recovery, 2) end up in an institution/jail, or 3) die.

I had a loving wife, good job, nice house, and two cars in the garage. All the supposed trappings of normality. But I was not living the American Dream; every morning, I woke up to a nightmare.

The fourth of the Twelve Steps of AA is "Made a searching and fearless moral inventory of ourselves" (*Alcoholics Anonymous*

59). We are asked to write down those individuals we have a resentment toward, what it is these individuals did to cause the resentment, what part of self their action(s) threatened (e.g. security, self-esteem, ambition, sex or personal relations, etc.), and finally, what role we had in the dysfunction.

My relationship with my mother surfaced as the primary reason for my addiction to alcohol, which I would soon recognize as a heavy-handed attempt to self anesthetize. I needed to thoroughly uncover the causes and conditions as to why I did this.

I began with the help of a sponsor (or mentor) soon after my sobriety date of August 28, 2006, and have remained sober since. It has been an arduous, spiritual journey: one that has kept me writing between bouts of sleeplessness, vomiting, and many other uncontrollable physical reactions, including many a tear. I am not ashamed any longer. I am a survivor. Yet, I tear up even when writing that simple line. I am, in fact, a wounded storyteller, and as Mr. Frank puts forth: telling my self story is a means of salvaging a shipwrecked life, salvaging what is there, salvaging myself and my voice.

I do this through writing. For some reason, though I have done everything to keep this part of me, which is the whole of me, hidden… I have been encouraged to write until the words fill the wound I now "walk around."

In reviewing my fourth step, my sponsor turned to me and asked, "Keith, do you believe you deserve *any* of the success you've had in life?" My eyes glazed as I realized: I did not. Mom had won. At least to age forty-four. She not only controlled me throughout my childhood, but the grip she had on my mind had remained steadfast. These steps I was taking, this program of AA I was working (and the writing), would be the watershed for its release.

↔

"One of our most difficult duties as human beings is to listen to the voices of those who suffer," *The Wounded Storyteller* advocates.

...These voices bespeak conditions of embodiment that most of us would rather forget our own vulnerability to. Listening is hard, but it is also a fundamental moral act; to realize the best potential in postmodern times requires an ethics of listening... in listening for the other, we listen for ourselves. The moment of witness in the story crystallizes a mutuality of need, when each is *for* the other. (25)

In a letter of recommendation, the writer was kind enough to refer to me as "a fine and decent man." Beyond any comment of academic excellence or other blather he might have mentioned, this small statement, an impartial and unexpected personal observation of Keith Thomas Hoerner, child-abuse survivor, gave credence to the fact that someone *had* listened (beyond the silence words cannot bridge). More so, that I *have* amounted to something, despite my mother's incessant admonitions to the contrary... And I desire nothing more.

*Works Cited*

Alcoholics Anonymous. 4*th* ed. New York: Alcoholics Anonymous World Services Inc., 2001. Print.

Frank, Arthur W. *The Wounded Storyteller.* Chicago and London: The University of Chicago Press, 1995. Print.

Kotre, Billy. *White Glove: How We Create Ourselves Through Memory.* New York: The Free Press, 1995. Print.

# RAIN

I.

The glass is stained
as is my memory.
Indelible.
The red of regret.
The blue of bruising.
The yellow of yesterdays
I will never understand.
So many colors call
me
to rummage
dangerously through them
in search of
myself.
Some memories,
sharper than others, mercilessly
prick
my fingers.
They are not through

with me,
but I am through
with them.
I see
the cuts
but feel no pain.
I am mesmerized by my
blood
dripping
on a blue sliver.
I peer closer,
again
proving red and blue make purple.
Today, I sweep up the many shards
of my past, moving
beyond it,
beyond them –
determined
at last
to make
one whole picture,
one whole person
from the many
r e m n a n t s.

## II.

After Mass, I sometimes lit a candle to commemorate my Dad near a statue of St. Joseph in a vestibule of the church. But this morning, I was drawn to the statue of Mary, the mother of Jesus.

I lit it there, instead, leading with a prayer for my Mom – and then, all those deceased in the family: especially Dad.

My wife, Anne, and I then left the church, met my brother and sister-in-law for breakfast and headed to the Nelson-Atkins Museum of Art. I was taking a class in stained-glass making, and there was a new exhibit on "Stained Glass from Throughout the Ages" I wanted to see.

We did the usual meandering through the rooms without purpose, when a particular piece stopped me. It was nothing large and spectacular; rather, it was a mere 20 by 22 inches: a small, centuries-old, stained-glass panel depicting Hannah, the mother of Mary.

I examined it, looking closely at the face, which had no lead veining obstructing it. This meant the artist was required to crush colored glass into powder, paint Hannah's face on the primary pane and then bake it – setting it permanently in place. A laborious task, it was deftly and delicately done. Eyes cast forward, there was no effected glance upward to the heavens or hands in prayer pose. Unapologetic, she stood not as some stoic biblical icon but as the human being she was. The frame of her body couldn't have been more than 12 inches tall, arms straight to the side, head and facial features the size of four postage stamps. She looked at me. Spoke to me. But what the message was I could not heed. I only knew it had nothing to do with stained glass.

We arrived at home around four o'clock in the afternoon, when I picked up a message to call my sister Jackie. It was urgent. My nine-year-old nephew, Ricky, picked up the phone.

"Is your Mom there, Ricky?" I asked.

"Grandma's dead!" he said. His tone keyed up, the way a kid might make it known the ice-cream truck is coming around the corner.

We humans can be terrible communicators. Too often, there is a disconnect. Then again, this was just a nine-year-old.

A day late and a dollar short, I believe for the few brief hours after her death, my mother reached out to me. After church. At the museum. A whisper calling from a plane of existence unknown to the living. Like a parched brown leaf in October, still clinging to a chain-link fence in a gale-force wind, waiting to say something before it is blown to hell, as I had just been.

At 70 years old, on Epiphany, the Roman Catholic Church's observance of the three wise men's visitation to the newborn Jesus, Mom was dead. How perfect for an Irish Catholic.

Ruminating on this, I had an epiphany of my own. He would have His gold, frankincense, and myrrh. But I would never have answers to my mother's absolute tyranny over me – even after extricating myself at the legal age of 18.

## III.

When *The Holy Bible* was translated from its original Aramaic language to the Greek (which would result in what is now known as The King James Version), there was not an appropriate word befitting the meaning of "sin." So they settled. Those translating agreed to work with the Greek word "hamartia," a derivative of "hamartanein," an archery term meaning to miss the mark.

Catholics are instructed to avoid any act adverse to acceptable moral behavior: to exercise good over evil. Too often though, according to religious dictates and the instruction of fire-and-brimstone pontiffs, we are left with the sense we have just one, maybe two times to get things right.

But the very nature of archery tells us otherwise. It establishes for us *a goal*. We take aim and strive to hit it. If we are off or entirely miss the target, by the very nature of the sport, we try again.

Actually, we try again and again *and again*. For here is presented to us a forgiving God, allowing the necessary "do overs" as we work toward progress, not perfection.

My mother, like most Catholics, was steeped in religiosity – though seemingly lacking in depth regarding spirituality. I fear she believed she had only one chance. Being human and sure to fail at this one-time-only walk of faith, it took her. Her personal aspirations. Her health through childbirth and alcoholism. And, inevitably, her life.

As a bi-product, it also put a very large target on my sister Kathleen and me.

## IV.

Anne drove from our home in Liberty, Missouri, to Kansas City, MO, after making the phone call.

Jackie had asked, "We're all meeting at Mom's house at six; can you make it?"

*Make it*?! I thought while looking out the window, aware of Anne's sympathetic eyes on me from time to time. She didn't understand the love I carried for someone who abused me so. Neither did I. Nor did I wish to face the countless times I wished for Mom to die. I suppressed this thought, pushing it back to my subconscious.

We arrived, and there seemed to be too many cars… the house… too bright for the reason of our gathering. *Mom, you were right,* I thought as I tentatively got out of the car. *Jackie is a Hoosier.* She had said this to me when I visited on what happened to be Jackie's 50th birthday. Jackie, one of the older kids, had just bought herself a convertible in honor of the occasion and had driven by to let Mom see it. Jackie was leaving as I arrived, but I got the gist of her visit. The door closed.

"Jackie's a Hoosier," Mom said, drawing hard on her Pall Mall Red cigarette, holding the smoke in with experience, and blowing it out with an edge of disgust.

"That's *your daughter*," I reminded Mom, appreciating her sardonic humor.

"Your sister Jackie is a Hoosier. A convertible at her age? She can't afford *that* car. *Hoosier*," she said between drags.

We walked into the loud voice of Jackie (all the physicality, ego, and self-absorption of Mama Rose in *Gypsy*) and the others. Nine of the kids could "make it" this evening; two lived out of town. They were gathered, some physically upset with swollen eyes, others carrying on in a manner befitting a "brew-ha-ha" at a tailgate party. Only here, there would be no back gate of a truck to drop down, only the oven door before which my mother died.

"Is that where she passed?" I asked my sister Beth, pointing to the floor.

"Yes," she said quietly.

"How long did she lay there?"

"For some time."

She then explained to me that Jackie had called early in the morning, around seven, but there was no answer. My Dad died eight years prior at the age of 65, so my Mom lived alone. Jackie tried again around 8:00 and then at 8:30, when she called my sister Kathleen and expressed concern. Jackie was always good at expressing concern but never showing it in action. She lived closest to Mom, about five miles away; couldn't she just get in her damned convertible and drive over to see if Mom was OK?

It took Kathleen to say someone should go to the house. Jackie expressed perhaps all three girls should go. Hearing this infuriated me. This wasn't a shoe-sale outing followed by lunch.

Why didn't someone get off their dead ass and over to the house to check on her?!

*Oh, Mom, you are so right about Jackie,* I thought.

They found her laying on the tile floor of the kitchen in her pink polyester nightgown. Apparently, she had woken about 5 a.m., made coffee, poured a cup or two, and upon resting the pot back in the machine had a heart attack and dropped. It must have been Maxwell House.

With her last breaths of life, she – like all – lost bowel control and soiled herself. The girls stood stupefied. Kathleen called 911. When she got off the phone, she and Beth pulled Mom by the arms off the tile floor of the kitchen and onto the softer comfort of the carpet in the dining room. A thoughtful but totally unnecessary act. They then began to clean her, not wanting emergency med techs to see her in this condition. Jackie, I surmise from experience, was surveying the contents of the house, while her sisters did their daughterly duty.

Beth stopped there; she saw I could not bear much more as my eyes flooded. Pools of salt water blinded me to ordinary vision and gave me insight. Mom had dropped to her knees, dying not six feet from where I knelt before her all those years and was beaten.

Was it by chance? Or was there an intended meaning here – by God's – or her own making?

My darkening mood drew clouded looks from my brothers. *Keith, he's sooooooo dramatic,* I could hear them thinking.

It was then I saw Jackie and Billy standing directly where Mom was said to have died.

*What's wrong with you people,* I shouted in my mind as I turned looking for Anne.

"Who's gonna get the ice box?" Billy asked.

Vomit came up in my throat.

*God! She hasn't even been dead for 14 hours and you're dividing up things? Traipsing all over where it happened! Disrespectful, selfish fucks!*

I turned to Beth. "I have to go," I said.

## V.

My three sisters and I sat in chairs directly across from the funeral director. *What am I doing here?* I thought. If anything, I surmised it was in case a decision needed to be made regarding aesthetics; "Keith" was synonymous with "creativity" in my family. Like a reverse compliment: something to be both appreciated and chided.

We were walked through the steps of the public viewing (or wake) and funeral procedures, then worked through the how-much-do-you-really-love-the-dearly-departed list of optional add-on services… leading to the all-important centerpiece: the casket itself.

"The wood or metal selected is of special importance," the funeral director said. "It will serve to represent the departed's style and comfort *hereafter*." I could sense my Mom's gag reflex pinch with my own.

*PINE. A simple, rough-hewn, pine-fucking box,* my mind flatly stated.

"Something dark, maybe mahogany," my co-dependent self piped in. *God, I was really getting to hate this part of me.*

With Mom's penchant for Ethan Allen furniture in a high-gloss, dark wood, the choice seemed obvious (at least to me). Suddenly, it was very clear why I was asked to be there. Apparently, I was more tied into Mom's likes and dislikes. I, even more than Kathleen, knew what made her tick (and ticked her off). Even in death, it appeared, I wasn't the only one who feared her.

Decisions made, we sat one last time in a row... in front of the desk... in front of the crypt keeper. I was staring too closely at the knee-length pink polyester nightgown being laid on the desk in front of me to hear exactly who was saying what.

"We understand it's customary to provide a slip for the dress, but we were wondering if you could put this nightgown under the dress instead. She was always so comfortable in it..."

So, my sisters equated Mom's nightgown with comfort. Well, I equated it with disgust. *Wasn't she going to be comfortable enough in that mahogany CAR we just bought her?* I couldn't get the echo of her voice out of my mind, constantly demanding, "Go get me my pink polyester nightgown." Which inevitably led to her hunkering down, *comfortably*, in a nightgown that was flat-out too flimsy for mixed company (even if it was her boys) in her chair in the kitchen, followed by drinks and a happy hour – or two – of *hit the house boy.*

In response to the request, the look on the funeral director's face was a tad wide-eyed and tight lipped. *Jerk off.* I felt the right to judge this request. His job was to keep his trap shut and take directions.

We signed on the dotted line.

## VI.

At around five-years old, Bruce, Kenny and I are getting the treat of a puppy. We are ecstatic as the day has arrived to pick him or her up.

After work, Dad corrals us into the station wagon to take the hour or so drive to the breeder to take our pick of the litter.

"What kind of dog is it?" asks Bruce.

"German Shepherd," Dad answers. He's a man of few words but comforting to be around.

"Can we get a boy dog?" asks Kenny.

"We'll have to wait and see what's left," Dad answers.

"But I thought we get the pick of the… the…," I pause.

"Litter?" Dad finishes the sentence for me. "We get the pick of the litter that's left. We'll get there soon enough."

We arrive at a farm with many outbuildings.

"Stay in the car; I'll be right back," Dad says as he gets out and walks up to a man near the opening of a barn. They shake hands, talk. Soon, he comes back.

"There… in the barn," he says, pointing. "Be polite to Mr. Johnson."

We scramble to get out and go running up to the barn. We say "hello" to Mr. Johnson who guides us to a pen in back.

There is a mother dog and four pups. Three wrangling with each other, rolly polly and cute. Off to the side is one… alone.

"I want that one," cries Bruce… identifying one of the three, wrestling.

"Nooooo, that one," counters Kenny. His eye on another of the three.

I stay quiet, because I feel wrong somehow for wanting to scoop up the one ostracized. "Why is that one by itself?" I ask Dad as he walks up with Mr. Johnson.

"That would be the runt," says Mr. Johnson.

"The runt?"

"Nobody *runts* it!" laughs Bruce.

"The runt is the smallest of a litter," he says. "Smaller, weaker, they usually don't make it. Unless they're given love and cared for lickity split."

He looks at me and winks. His bright eyes twinkle in a pool of scorched and leathery skin.

Mom's story of my being so much smaller than Kenny at birth comes to mind as does the correlation.

I feel Mr. Johnson's encouragement. But before I can ask to scoop up the runt, another is in Dad's hands.

That fast, the decision has been made.

Bruce and Kenny are pleased. They all walk away.

I stand separated from them. I look at the runt and sense fear for its future. And, even at five, my own.

## VII.

I was just seven-years old. I was in first grade, and the minute I came home from school I had to put a pair of socks on my hands. My brothers laughed and teased. I looked at Mom imploringly, saying "No, Mom!" Asking, "Why, Mom?"

"You're going to bleed to death. Pick that belly button 'till you're dead on the floor."

I did have a new, nervous tick. I now believe it had come from beginning first grade with no buffer of kindergarten. Whatever, I began to press the tip of my right index finger into my navel, much like an infant who sucked a thumb. It was innocent. Innocuous. But Mom had to blow it out of proportion, make me a buffoon with sock hands. No, there would be no play with me turning them into sock puppets. I tried, and regretted it. This was not to be light hearted about. I was to be ridiculed into stopping this habit.

"Eat," Mom said.

I fumbled with my form.

"I can't grab my fork with the sock." I looked for Kathleen. But she gave me the look that there was nothing she could do.

"Eat the damn food. That's all you get," Mom said.

I tried. And through giggles and imitations of food flailing across plates, I was able to eat some.

But this new practice of attack ate at me like nothing else at the time. Was she laying the groundwork for me to be her puppet in later years? In time to come, my life's servitude proved an act I found I fulfilled first with strings attached and then, even without.

In revealing this memory, it was brought to my attention that this was a remedy spoken about in popular magazines of the time… The periodic use of socks to break an unusual quirk.

Leave it to Mom; she used this as justification to have them on me from returning to school through bedtime, when no one outside the home could call her to task.

To this day, I prefer not to wear gloves of any kind.

## VIII.

I am in second grade. The teacher's instructions for making my Mother's Day gift are exact.

Fold and shape the Handiwipe brand disposable cloth to look like a shirt. Glue on the buttons.

Now, move to create the pants. When complete, join the shirt bottom to the waist of the pants with glue.

Next, cut out the shape of a head and two hands from pinkish construction paper with scissors. Use Crayons to draw my likeness: the eyes, the nose, the smile *my mother loves so dearly.* Glue these appendages to the garment.

"You do know where your head and your hands go, I pray," says sister Mary Margaret.

Cut and draw, then glue on the final element: a pair of tennis shoes.

"There, you have a beautiful, little replication of yourself, your Mom is sure to cherish," Sister adds as the class bell rings.

"Be careful when you bring it home; it's still drying, and let me know how much she appreciates it!"

I hope she will. A blue-patterned Handiwipe is folded for the shirt with a green one for the pants. I knew contrast even at the age of eight. The shoes are colored blue to match the shirt. My facial features and fine, brown hair are drawn with precision, though imperfect given my age. This is its charm. I am excited to have this surprise for Mom; because I could hear my brothers and sisters discuss their plans.

I carry it home gently as directed and finally spy a box in a bathroom closet in which to wrap it. For this purpose, I recycle a brown paper bag from the grocery store… The same kind we use to cover our books for school. I decorate the paper by writing: "To Mom" in big red block letters with "From Keith" and "Hapy Mom Day" in smaller blue-green letters underneath. Blue-green is my favorite color; a sand-castle dream, I would often long to escape to the vast ocean, build a real home with a real family… Why "Mom" is in red and so much larger than my own name is subconscious. I put it beneath my bed for the following day.

Dinner is over and Dad gives Mom a present of flowers and chocolates. The older kids dutifully splay this and that, proud smiles on their faces with the background sounds of ooohs and ahhhs.

I stand there. My heart beats fast. I am so excited to give Mom my gift.

I try, but I am brushed aside by another sibling and another. Finally, Kathleen spies me holding something and guides me to Mom.

Kenny looks at me surprised; he stands there empty handed. Mom takes the box.

"And what could this possibly be?" Mom asks. I have a hopeful look on my face that she will appreciate it as Sister Mary Margaret encouraged.

It is a regifting of myself to her.

But upon tearing off the paper with no apparent notice of the decoration outside, all I see are large, gapping mouths laughing.

The sound is slowed down, drawn out, unintelligible.

My eyes look again and see her flushed face, dropping to a box inscribed with the words Modess Sanitary Napkins... words I do not understand.

Upon pulling a fist of Handiwipes out, the laughter erupts further in unison.

As an adult, I now understand the humor. As a child, I am hurt.

I run from the room. But before I can break the circle of my siblings, I see my little cut-out head already severed, lying on the kitchen floor.

## IX.

A particular meal stands out. I am nine-years old and sit down for dinner. Mom cooks mainly in pots: spaghetti, stew, soup, chili. Anything that can be stirred up in a big batch for one and all. It is a reasonable solution. *And they are good.* I still wish I had those scribbled recipes on their yellowing, food-stained index cards. But they have gone missing with the other few favorable memories I have of childhood. Side dishes? They were few and far between. And dessert... rare.

This night it is stew. I am instructed to grab a bowl and come up to the oven to be served. I do. Then sit down. Surprisingly, we do not say prayers or such, everyone just startes digging in. Quietly, I whisper a prayer of thanks to myself as taught in school, grab my spoon and move to eat. The first bite is too hot. I have to cool it off with a few blows on my spoon. Also, I need to stir it up to cool it down even more. I move to do so. That's when I see it and freeze.

I'm not quite sure if I really see what I think I see, so I just look harder and closer. There it is: a roach lying on its back on the top – in the middle – of my stew. I am petrified. My eyes stick on it with the one bite I took scratching its way back up my throat.

"Don't just stare at it. *Eat,*" Mom says.

I continue staring. Trying to figure how the roaches in the house got in the food. I was too young to connect the dots.

"I said, *eat.*" Mom repeats. "You're skin and bone as it is."

I come out of my trance to see everyone else eating in a flurry.

My sister Kathleen nuzzles next to me to see what's the matter, when I notice I have begun to cry from confusion, wanting to eat (out of hunger and fear of making the lady mad) and not wanting to eat (because of the bug).

"Mom, there's a roach in his food!" Kathleen says in my defense.

My sister takes my bowl over to her. She readily throws it out, fills me another. This is one of the few times I can recollect a note of concern from Mom in regard to my personal welfare.

In pondering it now, I can only surmise the roach darted along the range hood and being overwhelmed by the steam of the pot, dropped into its contents. Lucky me.

X.

Mom and Dad had a ridiculously large custom table made to seat all thirteen of us for dinner. It's the only dining room table

I ever knew at my childhood house. I say "house" on purpose; it was no "home."

They could have simply bought a stock rectangular table, but this one was round with a clean white Formica top and matching Lazy Susan smack dab in the middle. Very functional, very convenient, and take it from one who knows all too well, easy to clean…

It stood on one chrome pedestal and gave the illusion of family *unity*, of easy conversations exchanged, the opportunity for all to share in each other's life, nurturance, and support. What a joke…

What I was force fed at this table of plenty was plenty of hate, abandonment, and loss.

It took a lifetime to digest, a lifetime to allow myself "to be excused."

## XI.

I didn't know if I just naturally had a flare for the dramatic or if it was a learned trait. Life at home was always such heightened drama; it was more suited for the stage and, now – it appears – the page.

I think back to fourth grade. My mind is heavy with new responsibilities. Before school, sometimes on a quick mile run home during lunch, and after school through to bedtime.

I hear the sound of rubber soles scuffing on concrete, high-pitched voices of a small group of 10-year-old boys.

I imagine the opening credits of a movie rolling over an aerial shot as we scurry by. It swoops down, pans us, focuses on our feet.

"Step on a crack…

And break your mother's back!" is squealed in attempted unison as, one by one, each jumps one legged through a broken patch of sidewalk to save his mother from this unfortunate fate.

I, too, denying my feelings – would often champion myself successfully through, putting on the brave face of an all-American boy. But I couldn't on this day. Letting the others run ahead (the camera in my imagination zooming in on my lower extremities), I slowly and deliberately jump on as many cracks as possible.

Everything seemed to be changing so fast. Kathleen raised me, but recently left home (graduating one year early from high school and eloping, which got her out of the house). Mom was on a rampage. Kathleen had escaped her grasp, and the control at Mom's core couldn't reconcile Kathleen could now live her life as she saw fit. Sleep when she wanted. Wake when she cared. *Feel* what she *felt* for shit's sake. But we both found this would take years and, for me, intervention. Most of all, Mom was terrorized at the mere thought Kathleen might end up living a life better than she. Unthinkable for the gentry Mom was or perceived she was. After all, Mom was married in a gown designed by a fashion house in Paris (*not Paris, Texas, mind you, Paris, FRANCE*), of which there were only three created!

Pete was about six years old and Brad one. The responsibility of rearing them: waking, changing, dressing, feeding (and then cleaning up the house – before I could get ready for school) was my inheritance, my newfound way of life. And I resented it. This charge ensued after the school day as well. I would come home and care for the kids as if they were my own: play with them; stroll them; feed them (with me eating between bites); and put them down to bed, often singing them to sleep. Then, I did chores like cleaning the kitchen and laundry, attempting homework with whatever time was left.

One day after school, the responsibility was too much for me to handle. Instructed to stroll Brad around the block for *two hours,* I circled and circled and circled. One stretch took me across the street of a friend's house. There – boys laughed, played ball, and called out.

"Keith, come play with us!"

"I can't," I said, low to myself. Brad began to fidget and cry.

"Come on, Hoerner…"

"I can't," I muttered, frustrated. Brad's cry became more shrill.

"Stop it," I said shaking the arms of the stroller. He continued crying.

"I said STOP IT!" I yelled, moving to the front of the stroller.

He was the most beautiful baby I had ever seen with a little Irish-leprechaun head. Now, it was red with discontent.

"I said stop it, Brad!" I yelled again as I took my right fist, swung it back, and punched him hard across the left side of his cheek.

The crying stopped, reappearing quickly as a pathetic heaving of his breath. I felt shattered, gruesome, like Mom. This is what *she* does, what I've seen *Mom* do.

Thoughts raced through my mind as I lifted Brad out of the stroller and held him tight. Strangely, a kind of paternal emotion welled up in me as I cuddled and comforted him.

"I'm sorry!" I whispered. "I'm sorry, Brad."

I walked him back and forth for minutes until his breathing and cries began to recede. I examined his face: no bleeding, thank God, but bruising looked inevitable. The guilt flowed through me. It was then, at just 10 years old, I became astutely afraid of becoming like Mom.

Years later, I would confess this incident to my brother and explain my fears of his becoming mentally impaired (chalk it up to the reasoning of a child). I remember his quizzical stare as I stated my belief that the worst had indeed come true.

"What do you mean?" he asked.

"Well, after all, you became a lawyer," I answered.
We smiled.

## XII.

I am brand new, but God knows – I don't look it. Standing there in my elaborately laced cassock, holding the most sacred of "hand towels" (surely a 1000-thread count or more), this new altar boy of 10 years old feels as though he might just levitate straight from the altar to the choir loft, as awed members of the congregation quietly chant, "Saint Keith… Saint Keith… *Saint Keith of the 'altar boys.'*" I am grounded only by the spongy soles of my tan suede Buster Brown shoes.

*Shit, why not?* I think. Catholics have saints for everything: St. Sebastian, patron saint of sports; St. Nicholas, patron saint of children… But, I do believe *he* was struck from the ranks due to a lack of evidence he actually carried the young Christ child across a teaming stream (at least – I don't see his medal in the plastic, carousel display case at the Catholic Supply Store anymore)… And, yes, even a patron saint for the most questionable of moral characters: actors. My Mom shudders.

Father Forester nods for me to approach. I walk, chin raised, handing him the neatly ironed cloth. He quickly mumbles a barking command regarding water and wine as he tosses the wrinkled mass of material back in my tiny hands with little concern. *I want to kick him, even if I scuff the nap on my new suedes.* I stand stunned, seeing the linen treated like an old dish rag, cupped in my palms like the limp, dead body of a dove. *Bird-killing priest,* fires through my synapses as I walk stoically to lay the decimated animal down and retrieve the water and wine for the sacrament of the Eucharist. I am worried, but figure Christ already died on the cross; so, what could Father Forester do with the body and blood of Christ now… really?

My accompanying altar boy, Johnny, lazily rattles the bells during the consecration. *Doesn't he understand the concept of celestial soundings? RING those bells! Wake those near-do-wells nodding off in the pews! Tell Hell that God has a new tambourine!*

Holy Communion is over, and we prepare for our processional down the aisle to lead the congregation out. I am to bear the cross, lifting the awe-inspiring hammered-silver art piece barely off the floor (as it stands taller than me already at five feet). I see Johnny still chewing on his host, and he infuriates me. He knows to let the host melt slowly in his mouth. *How would Johnny like to have his feet or hands gnawed on? Gads!* I think.

The crucifix is elaborate, the silver is trimmed in gold and the rod (comprising the bottom four feet) is encrusted in various-colored stones. They are paste, surely, but to my mind it has just been rolled, hot, out of the metal worker's fire through the jewels stashed in Aladdin's hidden treasure chest. And I am carrying it. Me. Yes, me. ME!

I walk to the front of the altar, look at Father Forester, as he nods for me to turn and face the congregation. Then, I begin to walk… first passing the "blue hairs" who arrive a good 45 minutes early to secure seats in the front… their crosses to bear? Canes of high-polished wood or dull silver aluminum, now regimentally spaced and hooked over the front of the pews… their collective perfumes as thick as incense, burning my nostrils with every breath… such that I can even taste it (as if a wad of hairspray is being shot directly down my throat).

How they stare at me. How important it makes me feel. With every step and every beaming smile, how the closing hymn ("How Great *Thou* Art," mind you) gains strength, and candles seem to flare to heroic heights. Amidst the singing, I hear the modulated grunts of Father Forester. Is it to slow down or speed up? *He's a curmudgeon.* I make my way, punctuating each and every stride with a sway that dramatizes every measure. Upon reaching the end of the aisle, I set the end of the crucifix down and stand there, waiting. Johnny will walk aside me in a moment and open the door to the entry hall.

I wait. A virtual minute passes when I turn with disgust at the fact that no one can seemingly do the task at hand.

The Devil and Mom walk aside me; both laugh giddily at what my ego has done.

I look over my shoulder.

Father Forester, Johnny, all the celebrants of the mass still stand at the altar!

That's why the congregation is staring, watching…

Unable to bare my cross and face the embarrassment, the ridicule, my religious zealotry gone in an instant, I find myself tossing my cassock to the side and racing home—never to serve again (which mom didn't care as she would rather have me home to serve her *over* God).

## XIII.

"Happy is the man that hath his quiver full of children," says *The Holy Bible*. One reason why I never take the text literally.

Thinking on it, I understand how my Mom's Catholic upbringing and its strict religious dictates (no contraception, for example) led her down the path of so many births: 13 to be exact, though one would live but briefly – and the other would be stillborn. This, nonetheless, left 11 kids to feed, clothe, and educate. (It is here that her understanding of Maslow's Hierarchy of Needs stopped.)

Whereas my mother was indoctrinated since childhood, my Dad was an only child, raised without religion, who became Catholic as a pre-requisite to marrying Mom. How did he feel about this commitment to children at the drop of a belt buckle?

They were World War II-era romantics who went the way of… I can't even say faith, rather the man-made law of Roman Catholicism. My parents chose to weigh-in against the scales of balance. He for my mother and my mother for whom? A quiver full of children was not for her. A few alone on Mom's arm made her ache. And the more the quiver filled, the greater her regret. Until she lightened her load, pulling-out the likes of Kathleen and me. She was supposed to nurture us. Keep our points sharp, our shafts unbent, our fletchings waxed and glistening, such that when released, airborne to the world – we would whistle down the wind.

But she took to target shooting. Down and dirty runs at God's bull's eye with Kathleen and me as her target children. Desperately, she tried to show God how His demands on her were unjust. The sacrifice this required would take its toll on those with the greatest of fortitude. What if one had the best intentions *but not the fortitude*? Simply, the bow would break.

No matter how hard she tried, we, her children, would fly wayward: missing the intended target. She would discipline us for wrongs perceived. Too slow. Too fast. Too humble. Too proud. Too soft. Too hard. Too, Too, Too… We became two splintered, two dull, two pathetic shafts in need of serious mending.

## XIV.

Amidst the hectic goings-on of all us kids growing up in a "traditional" middle-class home in Lee's Summit and then Kansas City, Missouri, times good and bad could be found. The good was just few and far between. A game of Cowboys and Indians in the blinding afternoon sun of the backyard. Games of Ghost in the Graveyard as dusk spirited in. And when the deeper dark of evening settled – the frequent muffled sounds of sobbing as a child knelt in front of his mother – being beaten, his paper headband with pasted-on feathers, bow, and arrows thrown haphazardly across the kitchen floor.

Having played an Indian that day, my mind escaped the torment through the fantasy of being tied to a Cowboy whipping post. My wrong doing wasn't the scalp found in my saddle bag; it was the matter of not using the toothbrush to scrub the grout in the bathtub as I had been instructed.

From the age of 10, I was not just abused; I was *terrorized:* physically and mentally by my mother. I could litanize each occurrence, work to wrench righteous sympathy. But I have more productive aims. Because despite it all, I have – and always will – deeply love her.

What does this mean then?

I have suffered perhaps more over the years by my inability to admit that love and hate can co-exist equally in the human heart.

This ebb and flow has kept me, a poor swimmer, paddling deeper into a sea of alcohol, self anesthetizing myself to utter ruination, because I could not feel justified to hate her. Well, I do. I love *and* hate my mother. And now, I know; that's ok.

I grow in my sense of serenity. I do forgive, but cannot forget, what transpired between the two of us. I have found serenity's first definition of clarity. I have freed my mind of its jaded cloudiness of recollection, tearing away the dusky shroud I have cast over another human being, maiden name of Margie McGuire, revealing just another person, like me, who struggled to make her way in the world, as best she could (or so I say).

Raised in an upper-class family in Lee's Summit, Missouri, in the mid forties and fifties – when the city was awarded the country's "Best Place to Live" moniker, my mother was the oldest of three girls and two boys. She attended a prestigious private school for girls. It was at a high-school dance Mom's junior year that she was introduced to my Dad, Derik Hoerner.

Just two years earlier – it was Derik Garris, for until he was 18, Dad took his mother's name, having been sired illegitimately by a rogue Italian believed to have mob ties.

All that has been whispered down the missing half of our family tree is that Mary Garris was called to the house of her child's father, handed some money, and told to go away. She took the money and left. Granted, it would have boded better in ethical terms if she had the means to refuse the money and leave. But that is apparently someone else's story.

Unlike Mom, Dad was essentially from the wrong side of the tracks. Supported by the means of a single mother (though eventually married to Warren Hoerner), he lived in a lesser desirable part of town and attended the area's public schools.

While Dad was on leave as a naval gunner in WWII, Mom was immediately smitten with his uniform and good looks. Even in the face of sounding cliché, Dad was classically tall, dark, and handsome. He was 20 years old, and she was 17. Mom fluttered about him, uncaring at this particular moment of the great socio-economic divide between them. Love can cure all! She was a cheerleader, popular, and with extremely good looks: a slim figure; the fair skin and green eyes of the Irish; full lips; and a thick head of shoulder-length, coal-black hair cut with the fashionable bangs of the time. Her dance cards were always full, but she shuffled them – keeping an open hand for Derik to cut back in at any time. Indeed, a uniform with a battalion of shiny buttons can blind the eye of any girl budding toward romance.

Physically, they were a perfect match. But classism was sure to prove the difficulty that would strain their marriage. What were the prospects of a man with just a high-school education? A good man who served his country at war? A handsome man who would return home a hero, only to be offered a job driving a truck for a national meat-packing company? Respectable in many circles. But could he provide Margie McGuire with the things she blindly believed she was entitled? Always a bigger house. Better furnishings. Nicer clothes.

Mom had gotten more than the 10 kids she and Dad ran around bragging to their friends they would have. What else could she possibly ask for? What else, indeed.

I can recall being out at lunch with a couple siblings and Mom about six months before she died. She turned to me and indirectly questioned, "I wonder why the Pope won't ok birth control." It was as if she was just talking out loud in a daydream to herself. Let's just say; I'm no reader of dreams, but the message was clear.

It's one thing to talk all free and easy about religious dictates. *Oh, we don't mind about the no-birth-control thing; we want a BUNCH of kids.* Kids come at a cost, as she full well found out. I recognize her sacrifice. I recognize mine.

I suppose her childlike look at marriage and motherhood was propagated by a privileged upbringing; my grandparents had a large ownership in a stockyard located in the meat-eating Mecca of Kansas City, which at one time employed over 10,000 people. Mom had it in her high-faluttin' mind she was going to "change Dad." To be what? I would find through my own experience everyone around her would be expected to deny who they were… browbeaten to psychosis to become who she dictated.

What a haughty, little bitch.

## XV.

When I was about five years old, I remember being woken by the sound of crying. I looked for Kathleen, but she wasn't in bed. She always slept with my twin, Kenny, and me: fed us, changed us, loved us, protected us. Though just a toddler, roles reversed. I sensed *she* needed *me*.

Kenny remained sleeping, so I crawled out of bed alone and followed the sounds: snaps and cracks, grunts and groans. I could not process them, could not find a place for them in the card catalogue of my mind. These sounds were new to me. But one day, I too, would find them all too familiar. They would not just be catalogued from known experience. These sounds (and the actions attached to them) would be given the ground floor of the library of my life. Its many-paged stories were the memories I would reread over the years, until I sought recovery from alcoholism, turning away from self pity and self loathing.

Stopping at the doorway of the kitchen, I found her. She was kneeling in front of the *mean lady who barked at her*. Having fallen on all fours, Kathleen raised her hand unnoticed, inches from the floor, signaling me to go back. Her eyes were wild. I wanted to hold her, take her hand and run away. She signaled to me again. So I ran back to bed and cried until I found a new escapism in sleep: something I would carry well into my adulthood.

"Slut," my mother said. Followed by a loud smack and the crying-out of a girl. The rest of the house rang silent.

## XVI.

Kathleen was fifteen at this time: 10 years older than me. She was the first of two "target children" in our family... me being the second upon her escape.

The circumstances that surround target children are hotly contested. For whatever reason, we are the ones singled out and abused, while our siblings remain relatively unscathed. We are the intended bull's eye. The arrow? Damaging words slicing the air. Soft hands hitting hard.

For me, I believe she disliked my effeminate nature. I used to joke with Kenny (our being twins and all) that he stole all the testosterone in the womb. This, *Mom did not like*. Perhaps, it was the influence of culpability.

As soon as Kathleen left, Mom's eyes narrowed down on me.

We were instructed not to keep in contact with Kathleen for fear of retribution, not to visit her, hell, not to *think* of her. Of course, we did but in secrecy.

"Keith, is Mom hard on you since I left?" she'd ask, the concern unmistakable in her eyes.

"No," I would answer.

I was never a good liar.

## XVII.

When I was a kid, I would sleep walk. I remember having a recurring dream. Today, it seems to be such a mature dream, intuitive and analogous, for a boy of about eight years old. I dreamt I would slice an orange. And nature would whisper to me that when one slices an orange it displays thirteen sections. Always thirteen. Only thirteen.

But the orange I sliced had one section more—or less.

I would begin to sleep walk, the gauze masking Lazarus' eyes bound tight around my own: making me maneuver the furniture in our house as if by radar, blindly gliding past hard corners and pointy objects.

My siblings, Mom, Dad, were use to my meanderings. I would find a presence, sense a group of my brothers and sisters as they sat watching Johnny Carson, hee hawing at his stand-up comedy routine. I stood there, too, mumbling, asking them for help in a language only the desperate can understand. "Why," I'd ask simply, pleadingly. "Why is my orange different? Why am I different?"

I would feel an arm drag me to the side or a kick in the butt almost take me to my knees.

"Go to bed, Keith!"

"Stop blocking the TV."

"Mom, Keith's at it again…"

A hand, assuredly my surrogate mother, Kathleen, gently guided me on my precarious walk back to the orange grove and the knowledge even then, on some subconscious level, that all was not right with me; something was wrong, because my surroundings told me so. I was witness to Mom's beatings on Kathleen. Just a kid, I was already sensing the dread to be caught up in Mom's manic moods. I had begun wetting the bed and being punished sarcastically by Mom on each occurrence. And the dream came slice after slice after slice.

One night, it took me to the place of the big "orange ball" we kids played with… when around two in the morning, Kenny awoke and went looking for me, finding me standing at the free-throw line staring blankly at the basketball hoop in our backyard.

I would surely shoot and miss.

I relate still to this image, me standing outside in the dead of night, head cocked slightly upward, blind eyes unlit by a phantom moon, while my mind connected stars like dots, hoping to map out the answer to my riddle through some astrological means. I could sense the half-horse, half-man archer, Sagittarius, lull me in my trance with the moral principles and laws of the universe... pointing his bow and arrow in the direction I was to follow, however far, however near.

## XVIII.

It is six-thirty a.m., and Mom walks down the hallway to the kitchen wearing her trademark, knee-length, pink polyester nightgown. A matching headband holds a short-cropped, silver hairdo away from a face slathered with three times the daily recommended dose of bright-white exfoliating cream in a single usage. She is not aging gracefully. A blazing red cherry tips an unfiltered Pall Mall Red hanging precariously from a thin film of Maybelline Beauty Blush Lipstick.

Mom has reached her golden years. The silver lining? She doesn't give a damn what others think. Period.

She pours herself a cup of coffee and sits in her throne: a chair at the kitchen table nearest the phone.

Mom takes her green "pleather" checkbook, an unsolicited gift in the mail from the KC Municipal Credit Union and begins paying bills with a cursive penmanship more apropos for a cotillion invitation – than a balance on a JC Penney account (to help clothe the last five of 11 children). She takes a long drag off her cigarette, pinches some loose tobacco off the tip of her tongue with the thumb and middle finger of her left hand, before she snuffs it out in a sea-foam green, 1950s-style ash tray chipped along the edges.

She is calm, in her element, more confident in her composure: a shadow of the self-conscious woman of a decade earlier... the modesty of a tufted bathrobe not required.

Back in the day, she would have been made-up for her audience of one, me, quietly eating my Cheerios swimming in milk, split down the middle by a heaping sandbar of sugar.

"When are you going to school?" she would ask in keeping with our morning script, smoke from a newly lit cig being blown in my face with each word – in the manner of Betty Grable or Betty Davis – whichever way you'd prefer to read the scene.

"In a few minutes," I'd say.

"Clean the house before you go," she would answer, again picking at the tobacco on her tongue.

Cleaning included vacuuming virtually all the rooms, so I'd jump up and rush to do the chore, or I would be sure to be late for the first bell.

This also meant Kenny and Bruce would catch the bus; I'd have to hoof it.

She had once told the only teacher who inquired into my well being that my only responsibilities were to her *and then God*, slamming down the phone. That call was never placed again. It was the '70s, and the Department of Family Services didn't appear to exist. As for the rest of the community? They subscribed to the "hear-no-evil, see-no-evil, speak-no-evil" voodoo of the age.

Coming home from school, Mom would often still be dressed in her night gown and usually on the phone, acting as switchboard operator between her two sisters, sans the switchboard. She'd point her delicate index finger definitively down the hall to the sound of two squawking infants: Pete and Brad. This meant "diaper change if necessary; take the kids out for a walk in the stroller for at least an hour, not a second shy; and I'll have a list for you, when you get back."

So much power in that little index finger…

## XIX.

I had so long been on the outside of life, the prospect of belonging to a group, any group, thrilled me. There had been mention of the Cub Scouts at school and an upcoming meeting for all 2nd graders wishing to join. I would get to wear a uniform, and this painted a picture of acceptance to me… a belonging to a brotherhood of similar interests (even if I would have to learn everything that made a Cub Scout a Cub Scout). The ability to do household chores and having no self worth were not skills looked at for earning badges. I could imagine myself in my deep blue uniform, pitching a tent, building a fire, doing "boy things," not babysitting and washing dishes.

One problem. One very big problem. An adult would have to accompany me to the meeting.

Mom answered my request with a guffaw, "The answer is no."

"Please, Mom, I really want to."

"I said, NO!"

I did not recognize at the time that my Mom was withdrawing from being seen in public. She had stopped going to parent-teacher conferences, invitations to get-togethers, even mass; so, why would she think to take me to a Cub Scout meeting?

"Can I go if someone else's mom or dad brings me along?" I asked. It just came out. I didn't know who I would ask, but I was that desperate. It came out without thinking.

She did not answer which in our coded existed meant fine with her; she didn't give a shit (as long as I wasn't on the hook for not doing my chores).

The day was here. It was so simple to get permission to ride with another classmate.

"No problem… my dad'll be glad to pick ya up. Be outside by 5:00."

I tore through my morning, lunch time, and evening chores with precision – making sure everything was just right.

I didn't want to give Mom any reason to pull the uniform, I was already mentally wearing, off my back.

I slipped outside well in advance to be sure I was ready. Excitement needed a new definition. I could not explain the way I felt. Concrete wasn't dull and gray; I could see the sparkles in the mix catching the red hues of sunset. The ugliness of beetle bugs crawling over Mom's maroon lava rocks had a newfound fascination as I was surely expected to be knowledgeable of nature and its surroundings. This night, I was hyper aware. Wound up and alert. Ready to ignite all cylinders in my quest to become part of this all-American tradition!

Dusk continued to fall, and I spied each sound of a motor, each headlight careening around the corner, each squeal of a tire. The wait was difficult at first, but when doubt crept in, it smothered me quickly with fear.

God, please, please, please have Billy come, I prayed. Incessantly, I prayed.

I could sense it had been some time, when in the distance I could hear church bells chime 6:30.

I stood, a small figure in the dark… no one caring to turn on the porch light for me as I waited. My spirit was crushed. The world was a vacuum. The silence was deafening. The concrete was again dull and grey beneath my feet. Beetle bugs, rolly pollies, anything living from the insect kingdom found the bottom of my shoe as I killed as many as I could – fighting back tears, conceding to go back in.

There would be no blue uniform. The only blue on me would be my aging bruises.

In a haze, I could barely breathe walking past Mom, as she sat striking a stupid salute at a stupid boy who wanted only to take part in stupid-boy activities.

## XX.

I knelt before her with my hands folded as if in prayer – as directed.

"You should have been a *girl*," she said, smacking me across the face, her head swinging upward, her voice stern, then quivering in a whining, melodic tone.

"Why do you make me do this?"

I knew not to answer. How do you answer, anyway? *Make me*? Make me kneel in front of her like God Himself, casting judgment – for what? Clothes not folded properly? Kitchen not cleaned fast enough? Her "marrying below her?" Not "being as rich as her two sisters, though she held more promise?" Her religion outlawing the use of birth control? For *bearing me*?

"You'll never amount to *anything*."

The alcohol wafted off her breath. Her hands were around my ears now, jerking me forward then back. I could feel the nails piercing my skin, something wet running down my neck. Able to float outside myself, I was nearly numb to it all. Though only 12 years old, I had unwittingly begun to build an uncanny resilience.

I dared not speak, but she deeply desired to hear me mutter something, anything, to give her the delusion of justification. I refused. I was a horse that would not be broken. Kathleen pleaded and cried for sins undone; I would not. She wished to take me to the floor, have me pass out amidst her frenzy. And though she took both hands together in one fist and knocked me across the side of the head, she was puzzled to see I always remained able to keep my shoulders from touching the floor. *Weebles wobble, but they don't fall down.*

My brother Bruce (a self-indulgent, pudgy, mamma's boy a few years older) stood in the doorway of the kitchen watching us like a primetime TV show. Kenny, too, looked on quickly, out of concern, and then had to leave. I often admired his brawny stature against my waif-like frame; his flawless, olive-Italian skin of my father, against my sunburnt, fair-Irish skin of our mother. He was my brave protector against bullies and questioners of my appearance at school, but at home – he was rendered helpless.

"Kenny," she called.

This startled me; she had never involved anyone else before. Kenny came back nervously to the door.

"Get the baseball bat from the backyard."

My eyes flooded, my mind drowning in the knowledge, that this time, she would undoubtedly take me down and for good.

Kenny's eyes locked on mine. *Read my heart,* my stare screamed. He ran out.

Mom grabbed my jaw and faced me to her.

"Now, I'll get you."

The kitchen's faux-cobblestone floor bit like razor-sharp teeth into my locking knees.

My peripheral vision momentarily caught sight of the Madonna and Child statue on "display" in the living room. Though Mom's and my proximity to each other was relatively similar, they held themselves differently. So serene. So–

A hit from the left. Her dominate hand. Just to maintain momentum.

Dizzy, I swore I could sense the kitchen – itself – begin to beat with a heart hardened by cigarette smoke, see the pallor of its face grow ashen from a soda and liquor river coursing through its veins.

My head, jerked backward, allowed for a single quick glance for Kenny out the window: the room's one beady eye over a shallow-mouthed sink.

Insufferable suffering was the slop served up here. The oven, ice box, and few cabinets ran along two walls. The rest of the kitchen's deceitful face ended squarely behind Mom, wallpapered with the print of faded flowers.

The longer Kenny delayed the better. I knew he heard me. Though, I believe he acted on his own accord.

"Kenny, get in here," she yelled.

Finally, he re-appeared... empty handed, "I can't find it."

"The hell you couldn't!"

She pushed me away, "It's your lucky night; get to bed."

About 10 minutes later, as had become ritual, I was called back to the kitchen and told to sit across from her. Mom cried, a fresh bourbon and Pepsi in front of her (with very little ice).

"I'm a bad mother, aren't I?"

I paused, thinking: *you're fucking insane; look at me; of course you're a bad mother!*

"No, Mom, you're not a bad mother."

"You know you make me do this."

"Yes."

"Go back to bed."

I moved to pass her.

"I'm going to stab you in your sleep tonight," she said.

This night, at the age of 12, I reconciled myself to death, confessing to the Christ child in the living room all sins and with His mother's help, somehow, someway finding sleep... only to wake with the early morning light by bolting upright and gasping for air.

Unfortunately, I was still alive.

## XXI.

Many nights, I woke up in a bed wet from drowning in dreams of the short life I'd live, dog paddling through runaway plans and getting nowhere, questioning my strength to swim the wakes of this erratic madness. With the first plan, I put myself in God's hands… figuring if I was to die young, He had other plans for me. Secondly, getting away seemed impossible as every route I ventured led back to a meaner, more maniacal Mom. Not far from our house were freestanding, one-day rentals, the size of a ten-foot by ten-foot room. They appeared like small cottages in an old Spaghetti Western. I would dream of somehow getting one and living on my own. The third option, bearing it, seemed the only rational one. That and killing myself.

Mom's ritual was to begin by grabbing me by the ears, while kneeling before her, and shaking me forward then back, forward then back. She would scratch down my face with her fingernails, and one day there was something new: hitting me in the face and head with the back of her palms. The hitting I could withstand for the most part, but it was made especially hurtful when I noticed her concerted decision to keep her rings on. Glittering diamond-and-gold brass knuckles. Afterward in my shared room, I'd lay still, everything feeling lacerated and loose. It hurt. The bumps forming from her rings, the blood beginning to coagulate behind my ears to form scabs, the hardening of my heart.

Once, I heard the front door open and Dad's low voice sound. Mom's dramatic, melodic, whining began: building to a wail with the liquid courage of her drinking. "He made me do it *again*, Derik."

Dad came down the hall. The door swung open as he turned on the lights. My stick of a body lay stiff. "Sit up," he said quietly. He was a strong man and took his hand and moved my head from side to side. He turned to go.

"Dad," I said.

He paused.

"She keeps taking my ears and—"

He inspected my head more carefully now, and I winced as he unknowing reopened the wounds. He saw the bloody mess behind my ears. From top to bottom: large red, purple, and black stretches of skin and blood. My eyes implored him to stop her. *For once and for all, as my father, as the man of the house, stop her.* My eyes welled up as he walked out of the room. His anger was palpable, and I felt vindicated. *Stop her; you are my only chance,* I whispered to him heart to heart.

"You need to listen to her," he said as he left. But it wasn't a reprimand. It was a warning. He feared for my life.

The Native American Cheyenne warriors revered their secret medical arrows as symbols of male power.

I looked to my father to be my warrior, to show his male power in my life.

Whereas, I used to hold him on some pedestal and Mom, counter, I've come to understand I harbored a deep resentment toward this loving and kind man for one thing. But a grave thing at that. He did not put an end to my mother's (I can never find the word; I pause, because the word is…) *terror*. He did not put an end to my Mom's *terror* over me. Where was his saving arrow dipped in the medicine I cried for? The defense necessary for survival? I was left to fend for myself barehanded and bareheaded. I withstood the blows. I rallied against the mind bruising.

## XXII.

Dad re-entered the kitchen where Mom sat smoking her Pall Mall Reds and drinking bourbon (what would, too, become my drink of choice).

"I'm at my wits end," she whined to my father. Yet, beyond the treble, the base of her voice scraped with cunning. Mom was manipulative. Why she felt it necessary to justify her beatings of me to Dad would always peak my curiosity. It wasn't like he was going to make her stop; she knew. He would exercise no control over the matter. He was clearly under her thumb. He would try and fail.

"You have to stop," he'd say as he sat in the chair across from her at the kitchen table.

"The kid's a smart ass. Never listens. I'll do whatever I see fit. I run this house," she'd say.

"I don't want this."

"You don't *want* this?" she'd say, slamming her drink down on the table and moving toward Dad, "*You don't want this?*"

I'd be peeking out the door of my bedroom in the hope he would be successful in some way, would be able to get through to her that it wasn't me she was really mad at. That she took her displaced anger and directed it at me. Now, I know Dad understood this and was saddened and embarrassed. For he felt his share of the onus lied with him.

"You bastard! You *bastard,* son of a bitch!" she screamed.

I closed the door, jumping in my bed and praying.

She smacked him. She continued slapping him through her rant, "You kept me barefoot, pregnant, and on the edge of town! I could have had *anyone,* ANYONE, and I chose *you:* BASTARD!"

I didn't understand why Dad took this. He was an adult; I was a child. Still, he remained seated and took her repeated hits and insults. Not until I was older did I understand the true hurtfulness of her remarks. He *was* born illegitimate. Or, to use more candid street vernacular: he *was* a bastard.

*Cruel, cruel woman…*

Once, spying upon one of these repeated occurrences and reiterations of Dad's lowly state in life compared to her pedigree,

I watched as he didn't even attempt to block her blows or raise his own fist. He sat resigned. Accepting the reality, the reaffirmation of his illegitimacy, I could feel Dad deflate, and I knew this warrior had no medicinal arrow to protect me. Abandoned by him, abandoned by *everybody*, I would mentally prepare to make it through the years that remained until I turned 18 – if I lived.

Controlling, manipulative, intelligent, powerful, a God-help-her-she-must-be-a-saint mother of 11, Mom stood victorious.

Walking back to her chair, she would keep drinking, simmering down, while Dad left the room to go to bed without dinner. *All* of her children were in line.

## XXIII.

"Keith!" Mom called.

As usual, I stopped whatever I was doing and all but ran quickly down the hall.

"KEITH!" she yelled louder, even though her peripheral vision caught sight of my ghostlike figure coming through the cigarette smoke spiraling around her, me, the house.

"Hand me that ashtray," she continued, pointing to the root-beer colored, glass square a measly 16 inches in front of her on the table.

I scooted it to her, stood for further instructions, and upon no recognition of my even being there – left.

## XXIV.

Mom, in an attempt to stop smoking and curb her soda intake, devised what she believed to be an ingenious plan: she would buy only one pack of Pall Mall Reds or one bottle of Pepsi at a time. The absurdity of this is that it was not *her* that would do the buying, not to mention it didn't work.

This weakness at keeping her plan resulted in unending visits to the corner store.

Upon seeing me enter, the cashier would just bring up the pack of cigarettes and bottle of soda from behind the counter without me even having to say a word. With that came an unwanted look of pity, as if to tip his hat at the craziness of it all. Too, he seemed to marvel at my always having the exact change. *Well, it wasn't like I hadn't done it a gazillion times!*

It reached the point, after awhile, where I paid for cartons of cigarettes and cases of soda – keeping them stashed in the back of my closet. I now had some money, having lied saying I was 17 to get a job working a couple nights a week as a stock boy in a liquor store. Of which Mom kept half the proceeds toward "household" needs. Think of it as a *reversed allowance.*

When told to go get the goods, *or just one of the two* (it wasn't beyond Mom to send me to get cigarettes, only to come home and then be sent *back* for soda), I often wondered if she was that absent minded or just hateful. I'd disappear into the backyard or take a walk around the block, anything to clear my head, release my anger, then grab the stash and give it to her. I thought I was so smart. That is until the night Mom proved I wasn't as sly as I believed.

I awoke, startled (as this was the only way I did) at the light from my closet and Mom knocking about inside. It was somewhere around 4:00 in the morning. And, the shadow of her body showed like an x-ray through the thin, polyester nightgowns she preferred.

"Where is it?" she asked, demanded.

"What?" I played stupid.

"Don't give me that; I know you have cigarettes and soda in here."

I was tired – and pissed – knowing I had run out the day before.

"There isn't any."

This particular moment stays with me. She turned and wasn't the aggressor I was used to. It's almost as if she recognized the inconvenience of waking me up in the middle of the night and the coming request to drive across town to a 24-hour gas station. Plus, I was 16 and getting older. Did that have anything to do with it?

"Will you do me a favor, and go to Quick Trip?" she asked, with a sincerity in her voice I was unaccustomed to. My desire for her love and the odd thought that this meager moment just might be the pivotal moment of change for our relationship grabbed onto the use of the word "favor," and I didn't pause.

"Sure."

Upon my return, she told me that since I was up, I might as well get going on my weekend chores.

Weekend chores generally included grocery shopping. On these runs, Mom would be quite specific. Her list would detail one brand of product over another or a very particular kind/cut of vegetable. *Canned,* mind you. I didn't discover real vegetables or real mashed potatoes (outside of the just-add-water-and-mix boxed flakes) until after I was married. I turned to Anne and said, "Damn, these are good; what did you do?" I remember, she looked at me quizzically and said, "Added salt, pepper, and *b u t t e r.*" Eyes wide with a fixed stare as if to ask "*what's wrong with you?*" What was wrong with me was I hadn't tasted real mashed potatoes – is all.

After hauling ass on a good eight to 12 large, brown paper bags of groceries – somehow, some way, something would be wrong on my return. Today, it was the beans. I was told to get French-cut green beans, but there were none, so I substituted simple, cut green beans instead. You would have thought I had done something truly egregious.

"Take them back right now."

"I'm sorry, Mom, they were out and I thought…"

I continued to put away the groceries.

"Don't think; don't *ever think*. Take 'em back *now*," she snapped as she sat in her chair by the phone, still in her nightgown. At least it was still about 9:00 in the morning, though she would often remain undressed throughout the day.

I had to be delicate; I didn't want to have Mom lurching out of her chair in attack mode. The only thing I figured kept her tempered was the favor I had done for her some five-hours earlier.

"I'm gonna get the cold stuff put away, and then I'll go."

Quickly I did just that, grabbed the four cans of beans and hurried out the front door.

As I was driving, I was fuming at my stupidity at trying to hedge off another trip to the store by selecting a green bean other than French cut, even if the store was out. For fucking 11 cents a can, 44 cents total, I was again trailing across town, burning gas and my patience, thinking how many times I had been to the returns counter. Then it dawned on me: *she really has you under control asshole. You've got a lousy 44 cents in your pocket. Chuck 'em out the window, and turn yourself around.* Which is what I did. It felt good, this little act of defiance. I also, if even fleetingly, felt fear that someone might have seen me. As if they could identify me, the car, and would call Mom. Today, I know this to be the imprisoning fear of those under severe mind control.

Returning home, I walked in to the smell of baking ham.

⇐⇒

I had just bought the ham at the store this morning. You'll understand the significance of this in a moment. First, I want to make clear the way Mom exercised her control over me. I couldn't just go to the store and be done with it. I inevitably found myself going here or there and *coming home*. Only, to be sent back for a reason such as the "beans" and *coming home*. Only to be sent out again and then *coming home*. Stop. Start. Stop. Start. Stop. Start. It was maddening. Still, *I did it*. Unquestioningly. I supposed I figured it (at least) kept me out of the house and out of arms reach.

Again, the ham... Dad worked many years as a trucker for a meat-packing company. He was now working as an independent trucker. While at the meat packing co., he got his hands on a great, industrial meat slicer that we put to frequent use. I laugh in remembering his consternation when he saw one of us kids go to the refrigerator and grab a hand full of meat, shoving it in our mouths.

"Use bread!" he would gruff. And rightfully so. He was trying to feed so many kids, and he wanted to satiate us on filler foods as much as possible, not fists of high-priced meat.

Nevertheless, Derik Jr. came by one day and decided he and his wife (and her extended farm family) could put the slicer to good use. *I thought that was what we were doing.* Regardless, with one simple request to Mom, I saw Derik high tailing it to his car with the slicer. *How fucking selfish*, I thought. *And why does she always ingratiate him?*

When Dad found out, he was furious but kept his anger close to his chest as not to incense Mom.

The required slicing of any meat for home had for some time now taken an embarrassing turn.

"The ham'll be done in an hour," she said. "Then you can take it to get sliced."

I knew this was coming when I first bought the ham.

"Remember, tell the butcher 'thin.' "

This is how it worked with the slicer now gone. Mom would bake the ham and wrap it in tinfoil. I would, in turn, go (each and every time) back to the store with the ham still warm and go to the service counter, explain that I just bought the ham from the store and wanted the butcher to slice it. Heads turned as the smell of fresh-cooked meat hit the air. A knee-jerk expectation of product sampling before sampling was even done in stores.

They were use to me by now and stickered the meat, so I could walk it back. I waited for the day someone would ask, "Why don't you just buy a pre-sliced ham?" They wouldn't understand that this *had nothing to do with ham.*

I'd ring the buzzer for the butcher, embarrassed, each time. When someone appeared, I'd nod—which between us meant, "Could you please slice this ham I just bought, THIN?" I was incredibly earnest about the cut, as this mistake could be sliced and diced many ways upon my return.

I always remember the kindly looks I'd receive. They would treat me almost gently (like the runt of a litter) as if to do their best to remove the awkward reality they knew I lived in.

I would carry a deepening divide of awkwardness and shame into my adulthood; still, the programming, the psychological abuse I received at the hands of my Mom was so entrenched, I can even recall asking Anne to join me to go check on her after

Dad passed and she was now living alone. I now ask, *why did I consistently go back to the epicenter of my abuse?*

I remember making the hour-and-a-half long drive hoping again to retrieve some vestige of an exchange, something I might be able to decode as appreciation or love, only to be greeted with "I don't have time to visit, but you can go to the store and get me a half gallon of Bryers Butter Pecan Ice Cream. My purse is on the table."

Of course, I was saddened – whereby Anne was irked. (She well knew my story.)

The store was out, and it put me in a panic.

"We have to go to another store," I said.

"There are other brands," Anne said.

"It has to be Bryers."

After three stores and no Bryers, I conceded. We looked for the highest-quality brand they carried, settling on Godiva.

Upon returning, the door was locked, so we rang the bell. I braced myself. She came to the door and stood there in the threshold, me pinched inside the storm door, the early evening dark a dull contrast to the one light I could see on inside. Upon explaining that three stores had no Bryers, so we had opted to get her Godiva, her eyes sparked, followed with her stern voice, growing in anger.

"I don't WANT it! Take it back."

"Mom, just try it; you might like it."

"I don't *want it*. Give me my money back," she said throwing the ice cream at my feet. The frosty exterior literally slipping and sliding it about...

"We paid for it, Mom. Listen, I was just trying to be nice."

"I don't want it!" she said again, as she rushed to close the door. But before she could, I used my right foot to kick it inside prior to the door's resounding thud on the matter.

*What*, I thought, *didn't she want… the ice cream or me trying to be nice?*

## XXV.

I'd often walk into my mother sitting in the kitchen on the phone. She would render amazing fashion illustrations freehand while she spoke. It appeared as if she did so almost without notice, the pen divinely inspired – tracing its curves, elongated lines, and flourished accents with little effort.

Standing behind her, I would watch fascinated. The sound of Mom's conversation but Morse code in the background, while my eyes traced the slope of her shoulders, her neck, her ankles crossing each other beneath the chair. *She is beautiful*, I would think.

I'd look again to the hands, curious at the enigma of how those hands, those elegant hands with their long fingers, could both create the truly awe-inspiring artwork in front of me and, if examined, reveal my skin beneath the nails.

Mom got off the phone.

"That's so good, Mom!" I would say.

For reasons I will never understand, she'd readily rebuff my compliments, crumbling the paper in a ball and tossing it in the trash.

"I'm just scribbling."

I never believed her; I took it as evidence of a talent denied. She put personal aspirations aside and married at 18 years old. That's what you did then. You got married out of high school, started a family, kept your home. It's what the Catholic Church expected. Women were to forgo the thought of worldly desires; though she secretly wished, I believe, to continue her education and study fashion. Design drew her and her it.

The family watched Mom's resentments over staying at home grow. It was a matter of religious dictates: of feeling her mind wasted, her talents folded away in drawers (feeding her inner anger).

With the distraction of time and family, this fire slowly smoldered – and all that was left was another smoky "what if" which seemed to haunt her.

Anyway, Mom was pregnant in tandem and, in turn, gave birth to 13 children in all: Derick, Jr.; Beth; Jackie; Jeff; Kathleen; Billy; Bruce; Keith; Kenny; Pete; and Brad. There were also two more after the birth of my twin and me: Calvin, who was stillborn, and Grace, who lived but the length of a prayer.

I often question whether fetal-alcohol syndrome played a role in their dying.

## XXVI.

In my mind, I paint you by numbers, capture your beautiful features one by one: from the fair Irish skin; to the coal-black hair; to the rich, ruby lips; and the fiery-, emerald-green eyes.

I reach for the pallet of paint and thrust my wet brush like a mop into a bucket and swish it around. To my surprise and confusion, the color washes your face with only shades of grey. The numbers on the canvas do not add up. I try other colors, but the same applies. A monotone portrait of shadow and sadness.

My grip clenches. My lips tighten with a sense of betrayal. I *see*, I *know your colors*. But reality intervenes. I see, I *know your lack of them*.

## XXVII.

Mom was a true beauty in her youth. With it came vanity. Sometime after 40, she began to use exfoliating cream on a daily basis. She didn't follow the directions on the tube, and I actually worried she might hurt herself. Her skin, uncloaked, was already shiny to the extreme and reddened (which I believed fueled her reapplication and grew her newfound obsession). I honestly thought she might peel back to the bone. The cream she used, though sold over the counter, was stocked by a pharmacist (to be monitored). It was intended to be used sparingly and remain on the face for only a brief time. Abiding by her own rules, as usual, Mom would slather it on and let it sit for hours. Her salt- and pepper-colored hair (more salt than pepper) was pulled out of the way with the help of an unflattering but functional, nylon headband.

"Keith…" she called.

I walked into the kitchen.

"I'm almost out of this," she said, pointing to the tube of exfoliating cream. "Run to the drugstore, and get me another…"

She paused, searching her wallet to see how much cash she had.

"…three tubes."

Taking the sixty dollars, I left without saying a word. It was always best not to speak if possible.

Grabbing the cream off the shelf, I was startled by a voice over my shoulder.

"Excuse me, young man."

It was the pharmacist.

"May, I ask who you are buying that for?"

I felt this was a tad rude; I don't know why. "*Me,*" I wanted to say, just to be a smart ass.

"It's for my Mom."

"Well, you may want to tell her to take a careful look at the directions."

I knew what he was getting at.

"Also, it may interest her to know she's going through enough quantity of this cream, we're actually stocking the product *solely for her.*"

The point was made. And I was embarrassed for Mom. Would I say anything to her? *Hell, no.*

I would be back by week's end for more, helping keep this nosey store in business.

## XXVIII.

In looking back at report cards, I am drawn to one from fifth grade indicating Sister Theresa's observations of me: "Keith is a very sweet and conscientious boy. He is always willing to help and is first to volunteer to clean the chalk board and erasers or anything I might need."

*Isn't that how you seek love? Isn't that what defines your worthiness?*

"I would like to see him participate in sports without the prodding of his brother, understanding that this does not come as naturally for him." *Great.* This, I recall, unleashed Mom's tongue on my supposed lack of masculinity. The remark prior... an obvious clue that I didn't have enough to do around the house – if I was so eager to clean-up around the classroom.

Outside of her short, robust form and rosy cheeks against a pale, white skin, the image I recall most vividly of Sister Barbara is her keen, twinkling eyes (surprisingly noticeable in the large mass of her black habit) as she monitored me.

One day, we kids sat on the floor, poster board and pastels in hand, writing out our favorite prayer. I chose the prayer of St. Francis.

Writing it out in a reasonably simple form would not be good enough for me. I would have to be better than the others with lettering akin to Old English text: decorative scrolls, initial caps in boxed filigree, details beyond the standard ability of typical nine-year-olds.

This particular morning, I was frazzled, unfocused from the "out-of-the-line" colorings going on at home.

I neared to the end of my project: only to deem it imperfect and throw it away.

Upon watching this occur once more, Sister Barbara bent down and comforted me as she could see the stress on my face, my shaking hands desperately seeking to get it perfect (whatever that meant). Ironically, it took me until my late forties to finally find that perfection is an illusion.

On my third try and self-imposed failure, I moved to throw it, too, away – when Sister Barbara bent down to me at eye level—a cumbersome task at her size, no care that her black habit was mopping up colored pastel shavings, gently taking my hand and guiding it to the prayer's conclusion.

"Don't be so hard on yourself, Keith," she said.

"But it's not right," I said.

"What's not *right*?" she asked.

I could not divulge.

"The… letters."

"Not right for *whom*?" Though I sensed she suspected.

She encouraged me to relax and find happiness in what I was doing – that God was there for me – and to pray to find the peace spoken about in this well-chosen prayer.

*Oh, Sister,* my heart filled, for I knew I had been touched by one of the first redemptive hands that would build my resilience and save my life.

## XXIX.

There are many reasons I can conjecture for Mom's erratic, unacceptable behavior. Sane answers to insane acts. A life of undiagnosed Postpartum Depression? Bi-polar Disorder? Another mental illness? Her unfulfilled self? Her lack of love for my father? *Her* being beaten or watching it happen to one of her siblings and thinking it ok? Something. Anything but the hurtful truth she simply did not love me.

I have been told, though, she would speak of me to others with a sense of pride about my career as an advertising copywriter: a sad example of our total lack of communication. She could never allow herself to give me a direct compliment. I discount this around-about sort of praise; according to Judge Judy, it is considered hearsay.

The question is: did we ever bond; *did we ever communicate?* When I was very young, even? I don't believe so. In a communications-theory class at college, I learned that if a tree falls in a forest, and there is no living thing around to hear: it *does not* make a sound.

The theory states there must be a receiver, some living being to catch the sound and facilitate communication, to realize and bring its message to fruition.

As trees fell frequently and frighteningly around me as I lived with her, I caught many an enraged message delivered with her hands through an unspeakable, physical kind of sign language I was unable to interpret. I know the sign for "I love you" is the index finger, pinky, and thumb stretched out to form the letters "I, L, and Y" but never recall seeing it.

## XXX.

Mom had been promising to take us to get shoes for days, but plans turned heel—due to her drinking. It had been established. Our annual shoe day was now to be this coming Friday. When we would go to the local Buster Brown Store and get our new pair of shoes for the start of the school year. Being as this happened once a year and my current tennis shoes had had it, I was excited beyond words. Especially in that Kenny and I were starting seventh grade at a new school, having moved a few months earlier at the beginning of summer.

I wanted to look as good as possible. I was a bundle of nerves as I knew Kenny would make friends easily due to his good looks and athleticism. It was sure to take more work for me. He had already made a handful over the summer, where I had only made one. I have always joked of him being "David Cassidy" to my "Shaun." Debonair vs. dork.

Finally, Friday came. It was the last chance to get shoes before the new school year began the coming Monday. No matter how many cancellations occurred, the promise of the day excited me. It really didn't take much to get me jazzed. Thinking of it now, I am surprised at the importance it held for me. Nonetheless, it did.

I began the day earnestly, making sure to hit chores with hyper attention. I walked about Mom as quietly as possible and only if necessary. I did not want to be called out for annoying her or giving her any cause to use me as an excuse not to take Kenny, Bruce and me to get our shoes.

I heard Bruce ask Mom if we were still going, and the answer was "yes." Still, it was early. Mom had yet to make the difficult transformation from nightgown to daywear.

The morning wore on, and then the afternoon. With the passing of time, my anticipation died down. I was forever mistrustful of Mom's promises. And when the liquor made its way out around 2:00 in the afternoon, I knew my hope for a new pair of high tops just slid very low on the totem pole of priorities compared to copping a buzz for the day.

The following day was Saturday, and despite hopes, there was no thought of promises made to prepare Kenny and me for our first day of 7th grade at the new school. So, I surveyed my clothes and put together an outfit, as did Kenny, for this important day.

Sunday came, and having missed the opportunity to get us haircuts, Mom decided to take this task into her own hands, literally. She cut mine first, wetting a comb and clipping away with a pair of sheers. I had no idea what she was doing. There was no consultation, no care for our likes or dislikes. She simply cut straight bangs, and the rest of our hair evenly around. Dreadfully, it was a classic Dutch Boy haircut.

Kenny kept quiet. He had the tools—it seemed—to withstand any possible ridicule due to his brawny stature and good looks.

You see, the problem was this: as a twin, we innately knew to try to fly below the radar. Being a twin was cause enough for unwarranted looks and teasing. But Mom raged through our clothes and told us what we were to wear as well.

That dismal first day came with the two of us looking like the logoed image of the chap on the label for Dutch Boy Paint. Same hair, same white tennis shoes (from the previous year), and even more strangely, white shirts under all-white coveralls. Two visions in white. Kenny got a taste of my world that day. His look to me was defiant in the face of my surrender. Still, he faired as I suspected despite all, while I was runted-out with barking calls of hurtful nicknames I would carry thorough to graduation from the school two years later.

## XXXI.

In just describing a memory of you to a high-school friend on the phone, I was startled by the sound of something falling… only to find it was a picture of *me and you*. A reminder that you're still looking over my shoulder.

I look at the picture; we are caught in mid dance, though appear as if posed, standing still. You have a smile on your face, which – over the years – I'd always told myself belonged to me. I now recognize it rested as a gentle kiss on Brad's cheek; after all, we were at his wedding.

Me? I was your dance partner; that is all.

I remember quietly fighting to get you to join me in that slow dance. You were reticent. You in the deep-plum dress you borrowed from your sister, having bought only casual wear for years. Your debutant days as gossamer as our hands struggling to maintain contact in a peaceable, non-combative fashion. In all honesty, I was no more than a cardboard cutout, a deflection to anyone who might've suspected a rift between us.

Both sets of eyes, feigning the flicker of a smile… hope drowning in sadness.

## XXXII.

Mom was not pleased with the amount of food I ate one evening. I was very thin compared to my stocky twin.

"People'll think you were in Auschwitz," Mom would say. *Lovely remark, classy, real suited to your privileged upbringing,* I would think. I was precocious; who wouldn't be who stood in my shoes?

I sat at the dinner table a good two hours that night, staring at the calf's liver in front of me, before I was told to put the plate in the refrigerator and clean the kitchen. It always amazed me how eight people could eat at a time (some siblings had aged out of the house by then) and the cleaning would fall entirely on a seventh grader. Sitting until 8:00 p.m., I finished around 9:30 to 10:00.

Yes, I knew what was in store for me. While my siblings were eating Captain Crunch and Lucky Charms for breakfast the next day, I was told to retrieve my plate from the evening prior. I did and sat down. My siblings just looked at me and laughed. The food was coagulated and disgusting. Mom kept her keen eyes on me.

My brothers left, their mess still on the table waiting for me to clean it when I was through. But, if I couldn't eat it before, I surely couldn't eat it now. I sat and sat. It was a Saturday, so I sat for a long time, watching the day tick by.

"Alright, put it back in the ice box," Mom said, indignantly. "Then (I know! I know!), clean the kitchen."

Why she felt the need to say that, I don't know: *cleaning the kitchen was a given.*

She emasculated me – methodically – by keeping me tied to her "apron strings," while my brothers were outside with Dad, working on the lawn or doing guy stuff. Now, I can say it; I hated her for that.

After another lunch and dinner, I was allowed to eat something else. Mom was none the happier with me, though; she could see my defiance growing stronger with age.

For *dessert,* perhaps the most emasculating thing my mother did to me was make me massage her with cream and "tickle her." She would sit in a lounge chair in one of her knee-high polyester nightgowns, the shoulder straps pulled down over her shoulders.

My brothers ate popcorn and watched the latest airing of *Gunsmoke* or *Laugh-In* as I would be made to tickle or apply cream to Mom's back, shoulders, upper arms, forearms, shins, and feet. Touching her body repulsed me beyond description.

I would have found it repugnant even if she did not beat me, but to be made to handle her in a way that pleased her, given our relationship (or lack thereof) was truly incomprehensible. It embarrassed me in front of my brothers; however, they appeared to think nothing of it. They were into their snacks and their show, surely thinking ever so briefly *better him than me*. They were, perhaps, too young to understand. I should have been too young to understand. But there I was at puberty, caressing my abuser's body, wondering over and over, *don't you see the inappropriateness of this? Do you even care how this makes me feel? How it repulses me?* Then to be swatted or smacked for "intentionally being rough" infuriated me even more. She demanded a lighter touch. Disgusting.

My wife, to this day, asserts these "sessions" as the reason I pull back at times from intimacy of touch.

## XXXIII.

Good times. Happy times. I search for them, but they are more difficult to surface. Yes, there was Christmas Eve. "Make-up night" when it was pretended all was well in the Hoerner household. But I would have to really search, if asked, to strand together the intermittent blinking of other given days (offering the unusual truce of this occasion). One would have to look deeply into the reflection of our drawn windows, to catch a few, unexpected sparkles of bright light.

Still, Christmas opened a whole new experience of fun and sneaking suspicion as we grew older. Mom and Dad, not about to wrap presents individually for a brood of kids, surmised an ingenious plan.

One of the older kids, I remember Kathleen, would corral us younger siblings in the station wagon on Christmas Eve for our annual trip to "Hill Top." An obscure road near home, it rose steeply and jutted far over a cliff: presenting a beautiful sight of the Kansas City skyline. It was, I had come to understand, an unofficially designated "make-out" point for teens. I, too, would revisit it for this purpose in later years. But I digress.

"When we see Rudolph," Kathleen directed, "We can head for home; ok? So keep your eyes peeled!"

We would sit in silence, our caps and mittens on (sans the mittens for me!), hearing nothing but the breath of anticipation and the occasional sound of ice crackling. When someone would shout, "There he is!"

Kathleen's internal clock would lead to, "No, sorry, it looks like a plane."

We would continue scouting. Plane after plane after plane. After all, we were looking in the general direction of the Kansas City International Airport.

Finally, with Kathleen spying her wristwatch ever so subtly, she'd concede we indeed eyed the bulbous, blinking snout of Santa Claus' leading reindeer.

With us jumping, physically jostling the station wagon up and down and side to side, Kathleen would quickly back out with an excited exclamation akin to, "If we hurry, maybe we'll catch 'em at our house this year!"

After a speedy jaunt, we swore kept pace with that magical sleigh… We bumped into the driveway, jumped out as if a hundred clowns compacted into a VW Bug, and raced to the door. Upon opening it, we would see a picture-perfect Mom and Dad smiling, and presents scattered about the room (unwrapped) with a name on each: Brad, Pete, Bruce, Kenny, Keith.

This was my happiest day of each year. Of course, we always *just missed* Santa's visit.

I would also come to notice Kathleen and the older kids (Billy and Jeff, for example), disappear into the background, their role fulfilled as I would fill it one day myself. For after eighth grade, the gifts stopped. Money was tight, and we were deemed too old for the frivolity of such childish antics.

## XXXIV.

My mother liked stained glass, too. And a large Tiffany-style lamp hung over the dining-room table. In my thirties, she decided to get rid of it. For whatever reason, I said I would like it.

"You take it down, and you can have it," she said flatly.

She always had a way of sucking the joy out of the air. This would not be a gesture of love. I studied her as she gnawed every piece of meat and gristle off of a chicken wing, practically sucking out the bone marrow. *Ok*, I thought. *It's not a gift, just me providing an electrical service, removing the trash with me as I go. Thanks, Mom.*

For seven years, I had it hanging over Anne's and my breakfast-room table. When upon moving, for reasons unknown to me even today, I left it hanging when we sold the house. I believe it was me subconsciously wanting to let go of the past.

Why did I want it in the first place? Because a lot happened around that light. Like a white-hot sun surrounded by a marbled-glass universe, fast-flying meteors (like arrows) often shot passed it: some able to be dodged, others hitting us dead on.

One summer, I remember Mom insisting the light be taken down and cleaned.

My Dad gently carried it to the backyard. He laid it on its side and misted it with the hose. Using soapy water, he cleaned it to a sparkle, leaving it to dry. But what he didn't consider was the heat of the late-afternoon sun. After about an hour on its side, I saw the fixture had bent to an oval shape... the lead veining softening.

With Mom napping, I ran to tell Dad what had happened, sure it would be the springboard to another unnecessary freak fest. I had a good meter for this. I told him I thought I could fix it. He looked at me surprised as if to ask, how? I took the fixture inside a far room and gently molded each panel into its original form. My life was one of details at a very young age. Mom had taught me *exactness* in every regard. Functioning in complete compliance is how I knew I could remold this light as I would one day find I could reassemble the very pieces of me.

When I told Dad I was finished, he came to see what I had done. It took his breath away. I could hear the sigh, though it was probably out of simple relief. Mom would never know of us nearly losing one of the house's few decorative features. It sat there waiting to be hung, instead of him.

Flickering in the shading of the light, a memory took me to a younger age, when six of the 11 kids were then living on their own, married or otherwise. Left at home, now, were five of us: Bruce, myself, Kenny, Pete, and Brad.

One night around seven o'clock, Mom went into a manic down swing and insisted I get her medicine. *Stand up. Walk five feet. And get it yourself,* I thought. Then, on the tail of my indignation, I truthfully feared for her.

Mom kept all her various meds in this large Tupperware bowl in a wall cabinet aside the oven. The only medicine I knew she took was from having her thyroid removed; the others' purposes... I had no idea.

Mom had been drinking heavily, and Dad was at work. She started muttering in late afternoon about how she wanted to kill herself.

A couple hours later, the self-pity escalated into screaming when upon her taking out the bowl, I walked up behind her and snatched it.

Mom pushed me against the door frame separating the kitchen from the dining room causing medicine to spill out over the lip of the bowl. I had two toddlers at my side, and I hurried to sweep up the pills before Pete or Brad might pick one up.

A chase ensued into an absurd "ring around the rosie" suicide showdown lasting a good half hour.

"Give me the Goddamn bowl," she screamed.

"Stop it; you're being selfish," I yelled back at her.

I kept being chased around that damn custom-made, circular, white-Formica table. This pissed me off. How I wanted to just throw the bowl at her and see if she had it in her. But I knew her not to be a woman of her word. I looked down, finally seeing and hearing Brad and Pete running aside me crying, so confused and fearful, it truly broke my heart.

Not knowing what to do, I ran to the other side of the house, told Kenny to call Jackie (the oldest of the kids living closest to home) and tell her to get over to the house immediately. Running out into the backyard, I hid the meds.

Through the kitchen window, I saw Mom stagger to her chair. I walked in the back door and took the kids, just missing her arm as she grabbed for me. I picked Brad up and cuddled him. Pete, edging toward the age of starting school, was drawn – eyes wide – to my knee in the living room.

"Jackie's on her way," I called into the kitchen.

"Wh-at f-o-r?" Mom stammered.

"To talk you off the ledge."

"*You* w-ill *re-gret* th-is," I heard her grovel among the klink of glass as she moved to clean up the evidence of her drunkenness.

"It'll be OK guys," I whispered to the boys as their cries and heaves reduced to hiccups, between large gasps of air.

Jackie came, and Jackie went. Nothing was said to me, the kids, or Kenny. I don't know where Bruce was that night.

I put Pete and Brad to bed and cleaned the kitchen. Mom had been put to bed by Jackie, and Kenny was in our room. "Good night – John Boy," I heard as the TV softly closed on that Thursday's airing of *The Waltons*.

*Indeed, good night – John Boy...*

## XXXV.

One of the strangest recollections I have is of the day Mom ordered me and Kenny outside on a Saturday morning. She leaned against the frame of the front door in her nightgown for the neighborhood to see. She had gone from class to crass.

"Get scrub brushes and some soapy water," she said.

"Huh?" Kenny asked.

"Your brother will figure it out," she said smiling.

We began to walk away to get what she instructed.

"I want you to scrub each and every rock that lines the front of this house: *individually—by hand.* Then, carry them around – and line the back of the house like this looks now. Understand?"

Kenny looked at me bug eyed.

*Why are you so surprised?* I thought. *You've watched me do this crap for years. Or had he? Did he ever really notice? Did he never really see?*

We moved around the corner when Kenny took my arm and stopped me.

"She's out of her mind, if she thinks I'm gonna spend my Saturday scrubbing down rocks," Kenny said.

Returning with the tools Mom said to use, I squatted next to Kenny who sat throwing a bunch of rocks in a bucket at the same time, then filling the bucket with water. I sat my bucket of sudsy water in front of me, took a rock, and began to scrub it. He punched me in the shoulder, knocking me back on my butt.

We laughed.

"What are you doing?" he asked.

"What she said," I answered.

"Are you a loon, too? Just carry a bucket of rocks filled with water to the back; they'll wash themselves by the time you get there."

It sounded reasonable; hell, I knew we could just take the rocks, move them, and hose them down.

"But she *inspects*," I whispered.

"She what?"

"When I scrub the grout in the tub with a toothbrush, or wash down the baseboards, or clean the floors – even on all fours – she comes in and *inspects* them. Does spot checks!"

I believed he was oblivious to all this and sat shocked looking at me. His dark-brown eyes blossoming into mahogany magnolias of recognition.

It wasn't even a half hour later that I turned, and Kenny was nowhere to be seen. I envied my brother's strength to show defiance in the face of the beast. I wasn't wired the same.

I went back to work. I wasn't about to stop or be caught not scrubbing the stupid rocks exactly as she wanted. Even though I knew something would be deemed wrong. And a beating was sure to be in store (they were always in the discount bin).

Her beatings had become her hugs to me now. A slap across the face was at least a touch. Human contact.

## XXXVI.

Another test of "mind *and* metal" would come one Saturday morning a few years later, though weekend tests such as these were standard fare. Mom liked instant gratification. It could be for me to purge every closet throughout the house: *in a day*. Wash all the windows by hand – inside and out – disassembling them and cleaning the storm windows as well: *in a day*. Or, as with this particular morning, when she woke me at quarter-to-five and walked me down the hallway whispering, "You're going to paint this house. Not over time but the whole thing: *in a day*."

I yawned, trying to wake-up as quickly as possible. I never liked Mom to have her faculties about her when I did not.

"I have the paint. Start here in the living and dining rooms; move to the hall bath, hallway, then the bedrooms. The rest will be up by then. When you're done with that, paint the kitchen, and move to the other side of the house. Be neat. No break but a half hour for breakfast, lunch, and dinner."

I awoke quickly thinking, *holy shit!*

"And be quiet about it. Everyone is sleeping," she said, before going into the kitchen to brew herself a pot of coffee.

Within fifteen minutes, I was working quickly and efficiently; at 15 years old, I was in a mental triathlon, my eyes on the finish line, which I would cross at 18. Then, I – like Kathleen, would cut the fuck and run.

I painted, "trimming-out" the rooms like a tradesman (finishing late into the evening), while daily activity went on surrealistically around me. I was The Unseen. It's how I lived in that house. No one wanted to face the nasty reality my treatment was terribly inhumane. Task after task. Beating after beating. Everyone stared at me, brows furrowed, as if to ask, "What is it you've done to deserve this? It must have been horribly, horribly wrong!" *Yes,* my eyes would answer back; *I was born.*

## XXXVII.

At 17, I asked Mom if I might audition for a play at school. It was a popular Neil Simon comedy, *Come Blow Your Horn.* I so wanted to be someone else. Slip into another person's skin, another person's life. I was shocked when Mom slipped, exasperatedly saying, "fine."

I auditioned and was cast as the male lead. Now, *for this* she was not prepared. "How much time will it take?" she demanded. "Don't think you'll be doing less around this house."

Two weeks into rehearsals, about one hour in length after school every other day, Mom marched into my room seeing me doing homework and said, "While you do your homework, finish the wash in the laundry room. And don't miss a thing before you go to bed – or you're out of that play."

*Damn it,* my mind spun. *There's a good eight, nine, maybe even ten loads piled up in there.* I was not in a good mood; I was tired and thought for once – I might have a reasonable night.

I proceeded to wash and dry the clothes, folding everything to Mom's specifications, laying them on the side of my bed as they accumulated. Two hours passed, and it was edging toward 9:00 PM. I was zonked.

Kenny was working at the convenience store this Tuesday night (a job I now split with him during the week). He got off at 10:00 and was usually home by 10:30.

I wrote him a note asking to please be woken up AS SOON as he got home: explaining my need to finish the laundry and its importance regarding my getting kicked out of the play and all.

Then, I quickly fell asleep.

The door to our room swung open, and a screeching wale split the air. Hands crashed down on me as the folded clothes toppled off the bed. I couldn't place myself; stuck between sleep and consciousness, I did not know what was happening. Lights turned on, and I saw the shadow of Mom's aging figure, her baby gut and spindly legs like a grotesque puppet behind a sheer scrim at the theater thrashing about in a rickety way.

"I knew I couldn't trust you," she cried.

I thought, for the love of Jesus, it's just laundry.

"I'm sorry, Mom; I'll finish it. I accidentally fell asleep!" I said, trying to explain.

"You're damn right you'll finish it; get up and start over. Wash all of this again," she said, knocking everything that was finished to the floor.

It was 2:40 AM when I started again, and I was finished just in time to make sure the kids got off to school fed and presentable.

Kenny apologized the next morning saying, "I tried again and again to wake you, Keith, but you were just too tired." I saw sadness in his eyes; but the caring didn't rouse him to help me as I worked through the night.

Leaving, Mom yelled from her chair in the kitchen, "Don't forget to tell whoever… you're dropping out of that play." There was such a gloating, snide tone in her voice. Why act all victorious? A grown woman coming down on a 17 year old. That's cause for applause.

At school, I sat explaining to the drama teacher how I had too many responsibilities at home and wouldn't be able to be in the show.

"I don't feel like you're telling me the entire story. What's going on, Keith?" she asked.

I denied; she questioned. Then, frankly, I was so exhausted from a lack of sleep – I flat-out detailed what had happened. Embarrassed or not. She simply looked at me quietly and in what appeared to be disbelief. But did she do anything to help me out? *Nada*. Other than letting me cop a couple hours of sleep on a chair in her office.

## XXXVIII.

We lived in a classic, 1970s, brick ranch with a large picture window in the living room up front. Some days I wished I could pull the drapes wide open and expose the craziness of what went on inside. Ironically, this thought was turned on me one day.

I was using the cushions of the divan (as we called it) to lay out laundry as I folded it.

In romped Kenny, 13-years old – like me, of course – and Bruce… edging on 15.

It was embarrassing enough to have to fold everyone's underwear, let along my mother's. Honestly, who wants to journey through the uncomfortable awakening of discovering his sexuality folding the underwear of his brothers (no big deal, really) but, more so, the bras and panties of his *mother*. All I knew is she had small tits. And, I do recall her saying more than once that, "More than a teacup is too much" to someone or the other. *Whatever makes you feel better about yourself,* I thought. Remember: this was the age before breast-enhancement surgery.

I don't recall the initial remarks, directly, but recall that Kenny and Bruce looked bored. They plopped themselves on the loveseat adjacent to the divan and looked me up and down.

Then, it happened. Something I was not surprised Bruce could conjure. Humiliating. Degrading. It cut to the core of me in a way I don't believe he... no, *they* could have ever imagined. For being kids themselves, they did not realize (I like to console myself) the hurtfulness of their prank. But they were witness to my targeting. And there's a Domino Effect. Children who witness the abuse of siblings too often interpret it as acceptable, an ok way to act out their aggressions.

"Let's make him wear this," Bruce said lunging and laughing as he grabbed one of Mom's bras. This type of thing I expected out of him and could have handled left to the devices of he and me. But to my shock and disappointment, Kenny – my protector – jumped in to participate. My heart sunk.

We wrestled. Them grabbing at me, me trying to fend them off.

"You're gonna wear it, and we're gonna stand you up and open the curtains so *all the neighbors can see*," Bruce chided.

It was a blurry, furious struggle as I whispered low pleas of "stop," because Mom was taking an afternoon nap, and I didn't want her to get wind of this and carry it further.

Once again, I felt weak and defenseless. Why were they doing this? Didn't they see, I mean really SEE what goes on? Didn't they feel I got enough? Was this *their* validation of Mom's constant remarks that *I shoulda been a girl?*!

I was down on the ground, face to the carpet, when they succeeded ripping of my t-shirt and putting on the bra.

"Please, don't," I cried quietly.

Next, all I recall is me hoisted upward, my two brothers holding me, arms outstretched, head slung downward like Christ crucified, the curtains of the large picture window opened, and the bright sun burning my reddened eyes.

They laughed and ran away. I slumped to the floor in tears, a stupid beige bra around my chest. I felt utterly betrayed. It seemed emasculating me was no longer Mom's sole right.

## XXXIX.

While in college, I would stand back and watch the students hungrily pounce on the bank of mailboxes outside our dorm's dining hall, push in their little keys, slap open their metallic doors, thrust in their grappling fingers, and pull out whatever paper might be inside (only to drop a piece or two or splay the entire contents on the floor in a staged act of clumsiness for all to see that *they* were missed at home, *they* were wanted). And look at this: a card for a care package to be picked up! *Jack asses.*

Eventually, when not being noticed, I – too – would walk-up to my box; though, it was well-known I very seldom got mail. And what did come was just junk. Forced to pass it on a daily basis, I'd look often – nonetheless, thinking *maybe, just maybe Mom might have sent some kind of token note or "care package"* (like the ones the other guys got). After all, we'd go months without talking, unless I called with some front for an excuse, only to get dead air on the other side. *I was not there to be her footman, her punching bag, so what did she have to say?* I reasoned.

Still, I imagined I would look one day, and like the others, carry the designated yellow card like the "golden ticket" in *Willy Wonka* to the window where the larger packages were stored. How naïve I was. Truly, how foolish and naïve.

When, upon opening my small mailbox, I only felt smaller. Still, even though I'd see no mail, no golden ticket *for God's sake*, I'd place my hand inside the compartment and rest it for a moment, feeling the cold metal on my palm, making its way to my absent heart.

I think of mail, now, because this is how I contacted Mom upon receiving a phone call from my Dad asking for a favor.

I had come home for summer break between my sophomore and junior years, after nine months of not speaking with Mom. I walked in the door and, *call me crazy*, was again hoping for some reasonably sincere "it's been some time," if not "it's good to see you," or better yet, "I missed you." Rather, I got what I should've expected from past experience and not wished for like such a ninny. "Take off that good sweater, and clean the house," she said. No word for nine months, *and this is what she says to me* from her kitchen chair, not even bothering to get up and look at me as I carry my few bags in the door. *So, she simply believes her servant has returned,* I thought. The reality of my inability to ever connect with her pierced the roof like a lightning bolt, nailing me to the floor.

I was upset, disappointed. Walking quickly, almost running down the hall, I grabbed the bottom of my sweater to pull it over my head and in doing so, knocked the corner of a shadow box with my right elbow, sending small thimbles, collectible spoons, and other tasteless gewgaws flying to the floor. It wasn't intentional, but I can't say I was sorry.

I heard a menacing caw and turned to see the usual picture of Mom in that damned pink polyester nightgown (*it was about four in the afternoon and time to GET DRESSED*) flying towards me. She raised her right hand, prepared to hit me across the face. I don't know where it came from, the strength to finally do what I did. Perhaps it was God taking my arm or one of his legions of angels moving it for me (because it happened without me sending any cognitive message to the brain). As she moved to strike me, my left arm instinctively rose, catching her forearm in my hand with a bruising thud. I squeezed it back toward her and could hear myself say in a stern, commanding voice, "You will never touch me in that way again. *Do you understand?!*"

More than the feel of her arm struggling to get out of my grasp, I will never forget her widening eyes like that of a fearful child: me kneeling before her, looking back at myself.

Letting go, she turned, flabbergasted – surely – at the knowledge that I had toppled her board game. She finally regained composure, if that's what one could call it, and mustered this much: "Get this house clean!" The demands, the demeaning language, the control, it was all ranted in one way or another. But I can say this; there were no more *physical* scars, no more brushstrokes of her brutality added to the canvass of my body after twenty years of age.

I took my bags and moved to leave. Amidst the firebombs of insults and attempts to reinforce the many reasons why I would fail in life, I walked out the door. Not only that, but I quietly turned and reinforced my previous defiance with one more promise, "Mom, I will never speak to you again *as long as I live.*"

A blessed year and a half went by, somewhat quickly, after having made a clean break from her. Though, I had phantom pains from the "appendage" I had cut off. Unknowingly, my codependency in regard to her and everything to do with her sick existence had been activated in my toddler years.

⟷

One day, I received a call from Dad.
"Hello?" I answered.
"Keith?" he said, hesitating.

"Hi, Dad, is everything okay?"

"That's… why I'm calling."

"Meaning what?"

"I don't know what happened between you and your mother…" *God, don't call that woman my mother*, I thought.

"But I have to ask you a favor."

"*Yeah?*" I began to worry and rightfully so.

"She's made my life a living hell ever since you had it out with her. I hear about it every day. Every night. I hate to ask this of you; I do; I really do…" *Then don't, Dad; please don't!*

I need you to get in touch with her; tell her that whatever happened was your fault, and apologize."

"*Dad, I–*"

"For me, Keith… I don't care if it isn't true. Your mother will never say she is wrong. Call, and apologize… *for me*."

There was silence as he clearly knew what he was asking. He wished me to walk back into Mom's life and re-engage her, grovel before her in repentance. It may not have been to actually kneel in front of her again, but psychologically, it was the same. Having lost her grip on Kathleen, the vulture couldn't bear not to keep her talons on me.

Not ready to speak to her, I wrote her the letter I so often looked for in my mailbox back at college. And it didn't take long for the speck of her to appear in the sky over me, circling.

## XXXX.

I sit in church sometimes staring at the stained glass, thinking of its origin. How in the Middle Ages most people couldn't read or write, so the clergy encrypted scenes from scripture into colored-glass panels for the people to take their "instruction" from. Visual crib sheets, if you will.

This day, I identify that among the many colors, I prefer the translucent, cathedral glass in gemstone hues, the candy colors: bright emerald green, blue sapphire, purple amethyst…

The sun slices the seam of a blanket of winter gray masking the sky, when a glorious break of day shines, momentarily lighting all windows facing southeast. I close my eyes, seeking the swirling kaleidoscope of colors as they blur through my eyelids, the sun warm on my face. I pray for God to open my mind's eye to the better times of my youth, too often usurped by self-pity, hidden out of view, stored for safe keeping under dusty shrouds. He tells me to be patient, for His saving grace is to present itself to me soon.

Eye lids still closed, I see emerald green, recalling a late-summer game of basketball between Kenny, Bruce, and me on a court poured by my Dad specially for his boys. Us flailing our hot arms in the cooler air of mid morning. Dad sitting behind us on a swing, head bent downward deep in thought, earnestly shucking a good two-dozen ears of corn for that night's dinner.

Sapphire blue floats by transporting my daydreaming to a clubhouse shared with the neighbor kids. Inherited from an older gang, it had a private stash of dirty magazines with naked ladies to last a lifetime. We giggled and grew up. Reckless hooligans, we threw dirt clods down from our hilltop position onto the road, hoping to hit cars like ducks in a rifle shoot at the carnival… no true sense of the fatal nature of our game.

The power of purple Amethyst drives me to the fast lane of go-cart races, where all us kids hand-built our own non-motored cars and raced them down the high slant of Belmonte Street. Over and over and over again. Sometimes, my rough-hewn, purple-bodied roadster actually won. Most other times, I'd fly unwieldy into a tree or neighboring car and rack myself, slumping in numbed pain (only to come out of it laughing in delight). I had my mother's sense of humor. A biting sense of humor.

The color of yellow Topaz appears and turns me maudlin. My eyes open, thankful to have recaptured at least three good thoughts about childhood.

I stare at the yellow chunks of glass and can't help but remember my bed wetting, getting punished as if it was something I chose to do. I'd beg Kenny to wake me when he went to the bathroom. He'd say he tried, while I woke-up in a pool of piss: knowing what was in store for me. Later, I was told heavy sleepers sometimes can't wake to do so – finding themselves wetting the bed when dreaming of standing in front of the toilet. I know now, I was just plain scared.

I start to put on my coat, feeling my mood change as the wiliest of colors dares me to stare. I walk down the aisle with my focus on the exit. But I stop my stride and turn. *Yes, I will say hello, Red,* I concede. My own reddened eyes from an all- night bender with my college roommates folly for its rich ruby glare. Mom's red lips, moist and glistening, whisper degradations in my ear, pushing me into the realm of hatred and pain. Irresolvable issues. Unattainable relationships.

"Amen," I gruff, kicking the handle latch to the large, decorative door with the bottom of my foot, finding myself standing in a sudden swoop of blinding, heavenly light that strangely envelops me.

## XXXXI.

I so want to recall funny things, moments to alleviate the melancholy of my memories, but I am eternally caught in the poisonous web of your personal tragedies, frozen, floating in the eye of the tornado of your hatefulness – and inevitable *eating of me.*

Still, somewhere between your fast, your frequent, your furious back-and-forth feedings, I recall *measured moments of reprieve* (an afternoon to play as a child, a conciliatory allowance to go out for the evening as a teen), where I could *feel,* ever so fleetingly, the warmth of you, the beating of your heart as it turned from crimson to black along each dying petal. This... but a pressed remnant of the love we could have shared.

You would have done me better to do me in swiftly, mercifully disabling my senses. But I was made to hang there, stuck and imprisoned with full consciousness, for your folly.

## XXXXII.

I didn't know (even when I left home in early 1980 and started college); I would still have Mom's marionette strings attached to me until 2006. *Wow.* What more can I say? *Here's to you: master manipulator!*

I drew loans and floated through a BS Degree in Communication Studies at a state college. I wanted to study theater, get a degree in escapism, but Mom said "no." And I *listened.* I honestly believed I had made it out of her grasp. Yet, I was paying for my own higher education and not living *my* life, because she said, "no." Looking at it from this side of the "looking glass," I was certifiably insane.

I was on the honor roll my first semester. Then, I discovered the school's sub-culture curriculum of booze, girls, and drugs. I dallied in drugs, but my taste for alcohol had a healthier countenance. After all, isn't that what you're supposed to do in school? PARTY? DATE? O*h yeah,* and study.

I didn't date much in high school, because I had no self esteem. And I sure wasn't going to bring anyone around *that* house. Mom used to chide me – saying, "Do you have any friends? You never bring anyone around…" I'd have no *words* for these remarks. Anyway – when I did date, briefly, a girl who I not only liked as a person, but sexually (she was without question: beautiful), I never felt comfortable, because I didn't understand why she wanted to date *me*. The *you'll-never-amount-to-anything, shoulda-been-a-girl, mamma-massagin' freakazoid*. Needless to say, I self-sabotaged that one.

At a college function early in my sophomore year of 1982, I met two young women I was particularly interested in. One gave me all the time and attention in the world, while the other wouldn't give me the time of day.

I dated Lisa for the remaining three years of college and one year after. The other, Anne, I would ask to share a lifetime.

Not too long ago, when asked why she wouldn't pay me any attention back then, her insight didn't surprise me as she put it quite simply: "You were too needy." And that I was.

Landing a job directly upon graduation as an advertising copywriter, I was a success story out of the gates. I liked advertising, and it showed. Treating each page like a stage, my productions got rave reviews, bonuses, and awards.

I put on an air of confidence, proof of my acting ability, yet literally shook behind a mask of fear regarding all matters of living. I was ill-equipped for life on life's terms. I didn't feel I fit in. I would drink to calm my nerves in social situations, because again, really, isn't that what everybody does? The answer is "no;" I have come to understand.

After I had been out of school for a year, and Lisa and I went our different ways… Anne and I starting hanging out. I was about to start at a new ad agency and can remember eating lunch with her, while she calmed my nerves about not measuring up to my next "rung on the ladder."

My life had been riddled with insecurity.

I asked Anne to marry me just prior to Halloween 1990. I remember carving a pumpkin from the bottom, cleaning it out, and slipping in the ring. Upon asking her to help carve jack-o-lanterns for my annual Halloween party, I remember getting a large knife and handing it to her. The size of the knife alone scared Anne. And I had to virtually hold her hand, forcibly making her excavate her way to the compressed coal inside.

When Anne completed the jack-o-lantern to the point where she could see tissue paper inside and that "something was up," I popped the top off the gourd and dropped to my knees. Since then, she has forever been my Cinderella. Through Anne, God has given me an abundance of love far surpassing any lack of it in my youth. We were married in fall of 1991.

My Dad would die 10 months later and Mom, 10 years…

## XXXXIII.

"Take the check or I'll give it to one of your brothers," Mom said.

This sort of statement made no sense to me, but I expected it out of her.

Anne and I stood there.

"Mom, you and Dad already gave us a wedding present," I said.

"No, we didn't."

"It was $1,000 toward the rehearsal dinner."

"Well, you need a washer and dryer. You just said so. So, like I said, take this check or I'll give it to one of your brothers."

This comment irked me. I hated when she copped a pretense like she had money to throw around.

Dad had died just six weeks earlier. Anne and I got married eight-and-a-half months prior to that. I felt blessed he was there for it. If here, he would have quietly taken the check and put it in his pocket.

I, once again, began to read this as an olive-branch moment – and took the money.

"Thanks, Mom, really."

"You're welcome."

This act of kindness made me uncomfortable, as much as I begged for such. It squeezed – put tension in my shoulders – like an ill-fitted suit, so I made some excuse to leave.

On the drive home, my mind meandered to a metaphor: how Mom (like a wash cycle) always believed she was bleaching us out with her Catholicism and Dad (like a dryer) whipped us into shape, sometimes literally with a belt at Mom's behest, to keep us from being handed over to her for worse.

Anne understood my needs, my seeking for answers where I would later find there were none. Still, she reminded me: the check for 500 bucks was just that… a check or 500 bucks… Nothing more, nothing less.

And I knew she was right. If Mom had an olive branch, she'd just hit me with it.

## XXXXIV.

Since her youth, Anne has suffered from chronic migraines. One medicine she takes required her to abstain from it for three months prior to the possibility of conception. A timeframe we are now well passed, the fetus (we were told) would stand a ninety-percent chance, or greater, of being impaired. She tried to make the break from this prescription many times over the years, but her health declined.

The thought of adoption for us was, in turn, squelched upon her diagnosis of Multiple Sclerosis. We resigned to the fact that for us parenthood was not God's will. When secretly in my mind, I wondered if He was protecting both us *and* the prospective child.

My mother's abuse had propagated an addictive behavior in me, backed by feelings of shame and rage. This was enough for Anne to deal with. I would not want the sins of my mother revisited on another child – through the sins of her son. I already point my arrow, aiming relentlessly at the mark of redemption for hurtful words, manipulation, and controlling behavior exercised on Anne over the first 15 years of our marriage. We now find ourselves edging toward 30.

In a salute to Dickens: they were best of times; they were the worst of times.

At the 15-year mark, as my alcoholism peaked – and I spiraled out of control, she sadly prepared to separate from me.

The ashes of this Phoenix smoldered. My soul awoke, and I recognized my life, the possibilities of my life, were worth saving. Today, through ongoing recovery, spirituality *over an organized system of faith,* and the extension of Anne's loving hands, all colors, radiant and shadowed, have created a window through which I can look with a new *and fairer* perspective.

I learned I was not alone. Sadly, every thirty seconds a child is abused; I am but one in millions! It was time to buck up, learn to love myself. Only then could I love Anne as she deserved and grow in our relationship. She had tried so many times to seek out help for me, to be there for me. I wanted to make sure I was there for her.

## XXXXV.

My fight for perfectionism was killing me. Mom had so entrenched in my mind that I would never amount to anything that I carried with me hidden *but heeded.* Who would have thought buckles – innocuous, shiny, silver buckles on a pair of dress shoes would take this fisher and crack it wide open.

I was, by this time, working as a senior copywriter and creative director in advertising and sales promotion for many years. Often called on to write proposals and make pitches, you would think I had a steely persona. In some ways, I did; in other ways… not. I think of a piece of metal, strong, unbendable, but when examined closely, fine lines, stress fractures appear. This was me. Seemingly strong but in many ways weak. The dichotomy was that I begged for the limelight, while at the same time hated it. Prescribed anti-anxiety medicine after the death of Dad, I found myself supplementing it upon need for presentations, etc.

Despite my anxiety issues, my strategic and creative problem solving was superior. Obviously, I had a naturally self-deprecating humor, which played well to crowds. Who wouldn't like to hear solutions to problems with humility and a little laughter in the air. It was intoxicating. Better still, it sold.

It sold so well in fact, even though in an environment where a person in my position was assigned to a specific region (North, South, East, or West), I was not; rather, I floated among regions, cherry picking high-profile pitches and program executions.

In the course of normal action, I was given a seemingly incidental assignment of presenting to a bank in Ohio. All went status quo, and I waited to see if we (*if I*, my ego and growing alcoholism was ever present) got the account. Soon enough, I received a call to come by the office of the account's regional vice president. She welcomed me in and asked how it went.

"Everything went as usual," I said.

"Anything stand out as odd," she countered.

I paused as I looked down at my shoes and pondered. "No."

"Well, the good news is we got the account. They found your strategy solid and the creative approaches unique. In fact, they couldn't disagree with anything you presented, really."

I wondered why she seemed to be hedging.

"There is one thing. And this is a little awkward."

"Yea," I prompted. *We knew and respected each other way too much for this 'round about bullshit,* I thought.

"They want us; they want the program, but they don't want you."

I was dumbfounded. I was the guy they called on to *save* accounts: BIG accounts. DON'T WANT YOU! buzzed in my ears. It took on my mother's voice, arrogant and unaffirming. How easily my armor of self confidence could yield. *DON'T WANT YOU!*

"Listen, Keith. It's a smaller account, relatively speaking, and there's more than enough for you to do."

"OK," I said. My mind scratched back.

"What happened?" I asked.

"Strange enough," she said, "Overall, they didn't feel your persona was in keeping with their corporate culture. The only specific I could get out of them was they couldn't get over the fact you didn't wear lace ups. That your shoes had buckles on them."

She looked at me embarrassed. Because, we both knew this to be rat's ass ridiculous.

I knew they were in *Ohio,* but the fucking Puritans wore buckles on their shoes. Lace ups? The only thing this tied up in my mind was the difference in me, the unacceptable difference reinforced throughout my childhood. I was hardwired to seek perfection… a perfection that would make me *acceptable to everyone,* proving Mom wrong of all my accused shortcomings… and I failed. I didn't know then that perfectionism is an illusion… that we may shoot for it, but should be satisfied with excellence.

I began to exit, when I turned around, having realized… "By the way, these are the shoes I wore that day." She peered over the front lip of her desk. "Nice," she said. "I'm sorry their buckles peeked out from under my pant leg."

These buckles needed a belt: a belt of whiskey.

## XXXXVI.

About three years after Anne and I were married in 1991, she encouraged me to go see a psychiatrist. My moods were manic. My anger was voiced loudly and erratically in the face of someone prone to a calm and quiet reserve: my Anne. Beautiful, sweet, and loving Anne. I was painfully hurtful. Coming to understand I was not as I believed (nothing like my mother), I recognized with an inner hatred that my tongue had become serrated just like Mom's. Sharp and getting sharper as I grinded it, tasting for blood. I feared its destructive capabilities: anger, manipulation, lies; no good could come of it.

I had gone to see a psychologist about five years earlier. I questioned the manifestations of my upbringing in my behavior and the amount of my drinking. It didn't prove prudent. I left my series of visits with the psychologist no better than when I began. Actually, I was worse, I believed, confused. I'd sit and talk – and she would *listen*. Seemingly… just listen. And upon leaving one day, she muttered something ruefully inappropriate. I will forever remember the comment: "I've heard of kids, going through much less than you with their parents, putting a bullet through their brains." How was I to process the happenings of my youth after such an utterance? I stopped going back.

Now, at Anne's request, I agreed to see a psychiatrist. To my surprise, I was assigned to yet another psychologist first, prior to being allowed before the great and powerful OZ.

The psychologist took me off guard; he was big and burly, and it was explained to me quickly he was an ex-Marine who wasn't much for bullshit or mincing meat. He insisted on dialogue, listened but wasn't passive. He actively listened as a means to question me further, deeper, seeking out the fissures he would swing his pick at – to split open the rock of my memory. He was clever. Amiable. Strong but not threatening. Still, I was apprehensive. I had been with his kind before and for naught. Still, I sensed, for whatever reason – he honestly wanted to help me heal. But why? Helping Keith was not an altruistic act I was used to. What was in it for him? Really?

I kept things basic for the first couple visits, which probably worked well with his basic-training frame of mind. Still, he played me. Got more than the basics from me, though I thought I was being guarded. Childhood abuse: physical and mental, resulting in extreme anxiety and fear. Low self-esteem. An emerging alcoholic...

"I want you to understand something," he said.

"Yeah," I stammered.

I can't remember his name or the name of the psychiatrist behind the next door. I don't know why, but I can vividly remember the layout of the two rooms, where I sat in relation to the psychologist, his brown-bearded face and fierce blue eyes focused on me. He did not judge... a feeling I tried to wrap my heart around.

I felt feminine next to his masculinity. This is how far my sense of self had eroded. I was overly sensitive, vulnerable, confused, and still sought protection. But from what? I was an adult now with no impending threat of physical harm. I sat unknowing of the second-by-second attacks my mind perversely and subconsciously yielded on my damaged psyche. The lead veining of my mind's synapses had been cauterized. My cerebral cortex would need a virtual reboot to free itself up: changing the way I perceived myself. My own self-hatred implanted by my mother would have to be methodically stripped out over time.

This was sure to be no quick fix.

"I want you to understand what a good person you are," the psychologist said.

"Yeah," I said again. It seemed to be the only thing I could muster. I was distrusting. Though 31 years old, I sat with the wide-eyed stare and emotional state of a lost 12-year-old.

"Do you know what brought you this far, Keith?" he asked.

I didn't answer.

"You have developed incredible survival skills," he said.

Strangely, I hadn't thought of it this way. I did seem to complete goals, make things happen, succeed. But I also self-sabotaged many successes, due to a deep-seated sense it was undeserving. After all, I had been programmed that I "would never amount to anything."

"Want to know something else?" He added. "And I mean this, Keith. If I ever went back to war and could pick just one person to share a foxhole with – I'd want *you* at my back."

I remember being moved and still take great pride in this remark. It gave me strength, didn't make me feel so weak. I knew he was right, that I had inherently high survival skills. I was the veritable walking dead. Zombie of zombies! But this remark reaffirmed me, re-inflated my soul with the breath of trust.

It was the first plank on a bridge to finding myself on the shore of normalcy. If there is such a thing. If anything, I began to see myself worth a dime, maybe a nickel more.

Diagnosed with post-traumatic stress disorder, the psychiatrist did his job of writing-out prescriptions for anxiety, depression, not to mention something to stave off my excessive drinking. Designed to make one vomit upon drinking alcohol, I found I could drink beyond moderation despite it, feeling no ill side effects. Though, deep inside, I knew this to be a serious warning of my growth into full-blown alcoholism, I secretly laughed at its ineffectiveness over me.

## XXXXVII.

Today it sits barren and boarded up, like a vacated movie set. The Barber Shop's red- and white-striped pole no longer turns, inviting fathers to bring their sons in for first haircuts.

The windows of the then Ben Franklin Five & Dime are frosted over with years of grit and grime... The empty shelves longing to be full again with bright-colored yo-yos, bubblegum, and summer flip-flops.

The Beauty Shop needs a facelift; the Liquor Store sits in its own stupor – a visual hangover of a time long gone.

This is where I, when allowed out of the house, hung as a budding nine year old, having begged my mother to allow me to walk the two miles. Highland Village was the hub where everything happened and where nothing went on now.

I am driving the old haunts in preparation for what you read. Ghost-like, I see a strip of butcher-block paper hanging on the inside-front window of the Meat-City Market: hawking ground chuck for 79 cents a pound. Its red-marker handwriting sun bleached and difficult to read.

I scan the horizon for my paper stand: which stood across the parking lot at the intersection of Highland and Sunflower Drive. It appears gone, but I walk to the location anyhow. One piece of rusting, gray metal lays flattened, smashed to the ground, where the two-shelved stand once stood. I can, to my surprise, still see the burn marks in the asphalt –where I had kids freeze, circled them in lighter fluid, then lit it aflame – to watch them standing in a burning circle of fire. There unexpected fear rising in the flickering reflections of their eyes seemed funny to me then (given Mom's influence of hurt). Today, I see the cruelty of it.

Their reward for bearing the brunt of my joke: a mere five cents… ill spent on my part. I could have used my Marine psychologist back then…

I looked toward the Five & Dime, identifying the spatial difference perceived by a nine-year-old child versus an adult. The parking lot is not at all as large as it had seemed. I envision a momentary bustle of activity at its center, remembering the summer I snuck in and stole a pair of sandals. Days, long stretches of minutes coveting them in the window in the heat of the summer sun, come back to me. *What was it?* I ask myself, *that made me desire them so.* It is mostly shadow today, but the salivating nature, the absolute sense that I must have them, I can still feel in my gut. Perhaps it stemmed from having "shoe day" once a year as explained. I only had a traditional pair of tennis shoes. This was something new: wearing shoes but feeling barefoot. So, a pair found their way into my zippered, vinyl, plaid, school-issue bookbag of the early '70s, and I left.

Now, the irony is I couldn't wear them whereby anyone in my family, especially Mom, would see them. For all new which one pair of shoes I wore. I kept them sandals, the flip flops, hidden, and took them out to wear momentarily on the walk home from school, while pushing Brad around the block in the stroller, whenever I could for the first one or two days after taking them.

Still, with Catholic guilt kickin' in, I confessed their theft in my weekly confession at school. I was reminded of the sinfulness of my act and instructed as part of my penance to take them back to the store, speak to the manager, admit to my stealing them, and bear the consequences.

I did as he said, though begrudging out of fear. The manager, sensing my understanding of the wrongfulness of my deed, told me he would take them back and, to my surprise and delight, would not call my parents as long as I found my way by the store for one hour of work a week to clean up in the back room for what summer break remained.

In reflecting, across barren buildings and broken glass, I again feel the palpable heartbeat of that priest and store manager becoming two more stepping stones toward socialization and responsible codes of action. From the likes of them, I was being nurtured (not condemned); I was beginning to understand the concept of understanding.

I now comprehend, it was wrong to pay five cents to hear a child, any other child *but me*, scream.

I also understood, it was right to return what was not mine, for in doing so, my moral compass was shown the direction of true north.

## XXXXVIII.

In my young marriage, I would continue to trek the 55 miles from Anne's and my house to visit Mom, since all the kids had run away after Dad died.

What I wished for was some conversation, that slim chance answers might be shared regarding our tenuous (oh, let's just say Shit-Show) relationship and get to the truth of it. I'd appear, say "hello," and she'd just counter with, "Go to the store; here's my list and the money. Put the groceries away when you get back, and lay the change on the table near my purse. I'm taking a nap." All illusions of her once being a lady with a lick of courtesy were, well, gone. Truly, pictures are one thing. But "the proof's in the pudding" as Mom used to say, and this pudding sucked.

The sad thing? I was so codependent, I'd do it. Again and again, the same routine. Until one day, I couldn't make the long ride just to do her bidding.

Before stopping, after saying "hello" and standing within that usual pregnant pause, pun *intended*, I asked her, "Mom, why did you do what you did to me all those years?" *I couldn't even be direct about it.*

"What?" she said, looking partly up, eyes cast downward, the epitome of confused age and frailty.

*Don't you dare get old on me, pull out the Alzheimer's card!* I thought.

"What do you mean, what?" I ping-ponged back at her.

"I was a slave in this house, a beaten-down, frightened child who you abused."

"What are you talking about?" she repeated.

"Oh, for God's sake, Mom! What is it about me you hated so much?"

"You want to know why I depended on you?" her head snapped up, eyes full and wide, lips on fire. "I depended on YOU, because I knew if I told YOU to do something it would get done and right! I couldn't get that from Bruce or Kenny. I *depended* on YOU is all."

I had to leave; I was feeling sick and figured she could get her own fake, feeble ass to the store.

As I backed out of the driveway, I nearly took out the trash cans in the front of the house. Not even making it a mile, I had to pull off to the side of the road. Chaos raged through my mind, my body shook convulsively: *she deflects and minimizes all the years I suffered at her hands to fucking dependence on me? For doing things she claims others would not do as well?*

*Torture them the way you did me, Mom, and you'll find one's tune changes quickly.* Oh God, I hated myself for what I was thinking, but I couldn't help it: *you should have spread the Goddamn wealth!*

I jerked the car in drive and peeled back on the road. It was all a bunch of self-justifying, what-are-you-talking-about lies anyhow. If it wasn't for the old-lady routine she worked so well these days, I felt a breath away from turning around and dragging her from one side of the house to the other by her hair. Just to give her a taste of what I was talking about. That might jog her memory. I swear; I could have killed the bitch!

It was suppose to be *me* depending on *her*...

## XXXXIX.

I may have laid a slat or two on a bridge to a better me, but I would find myself head over heels in liquor before I found I would have to swim my way out of it to reach the other side, literally.

In a drunken stupor, I would later fall in the street and obliterate my right ankle. I remember lying on brick pavers with my body contorted and my right foot pointing in the opposite direction it was intended. I was in shock... my vision blurry, noticing the shadows of people walking by, not stopping to help.

I felt like the beaten man left on the side of the road in *The Bible's* parable of the Good Samaritan. Would there be one for me? Two, three people glanced and passed. *Finally,* someone stopped. I mumbled for him to please go to my car, where I pointed, and get my cell phone to call an ambulance. He surely only heard a drunken mumbling.

All I know is an ambulance did arrive.

While driving to the hospital, I recall being asked if I had consumed any alcohol. "A-cou-ple," I slurred. A drunk's programmed response. I remember the surgeon telling me, "I didn't know what I was looking at," when he first examined the x-rays of my ankle. It required nine screws and two steel plates to reassemble and months of rehab.

That night, I literally hit rock bottom – falling with my face against the unforgiving cold of the cobblestone street (like Mom when she died on the tile of the kitchen floor). But as "The Big Book" of AA explains when speaking of sanity: a jaywalker strolls across the street and gets clipped. Still, he's a jaywalker and does it again… and again he gets clipped. He does it again – and keeps doing it again – until he's clipped one final time: killing himself. This is an act of insanity; the doing of an act over and over again, knowing the result, but expecting a different outcome.

My recovery from alcoholism began August 28th of 2006, after a fourth DWI charge and a night handcuffed to a bench in the Clay County, Missouri, police station.

Two previous charges were plea-bargained down to the likes of careless-and-imprudent driving (akin to a "rolling stop") with the third resulting in an all-out DWI and a one-year license revocation. This had me saying, "I'll never drink and drive again." But having drunk everything in the house this night, I figured I could manage driving the two miles to the "corner" bar.

It was so close, I could have walked. Still, on this night, August 27, 2006, I was stopped for my fourth DWI charge. This one stuck, too, as was well deserved.

The laws, however, changed just two days after, which saved my ass. The law now elevated any plea-bargained charge up to its full consequences. In other words, if I had gotten the DWI after the 29$^{th}$, when the prosecuting attorney and judge looked at my driving record, they would not be assessing two careless and imprudent charges and two DWIs, they would be looking at four DWIs and imminent prison time.

With only two DWIs being looked at because I (by the grace of God) received the ticket two days earlier, prior to the law change – I still faced prison time but not as much.

I was numb, my mind dark with fear.

I admitted myself into an outpatient alcohol abuse program at a local hospital in order to "look better" for the courts. But somehow, despite a few previous, brief attempts at sobriety, I opened my being to the reality of my disease. My Mom's disease. And that of many in my family.

Unknowingly, whereas I believed myself to be religious and God fearing, I soon learned I did not have God in my life. He had carried me safely, though undoubtedly wounded, throughout my childhood. But at the age of 18, upon extricating myself from the prison I thought of as home, I pushed God to the wayside, and drove headfirst into a new world of immediate gratification and recklessness that had no place for the likes of God.

It was my time. Everything revolved around me and my wants. I behaved like an unfed animal. Yes, I could be kind. Yes, I could be perceived as a good person. And, yes, I could be both. But I was also self absorbed… So hungry was I, so thirsty for the taste of freedom after so many years of captivity.

This hunger would grow insatiable, until I embraced AA 26 years later. Something I used to wish my mother would have done in her lifetime. But where she and I are considered, I've grown up and stopped wishing.

I can now deal with what's *real*, living life on life's terms. Most days.

## XXXXX.

My side of the family celebrated Christmas 2000 at my sister Beth's house. Mom sat against a corner wall quietly watching, taking everything in. Her body seemed to palpably resonate with the sights and sounds she processed.

I sensed her time was near, and she knew it.

It is in this manner which my Dad acted at a family gathering at Kenny's house just days before he passed.

I asked Mom if she had eaten. She said, "No." So, I went and made a plate for her that she could take home. Upon setting it beside her, I told her I included some of a new cucumber salad I had made from an award-winning recipe out of Dallas. She wasn't listening. But I knew she'd like it; we had the same palate.

"Mom?" I said.

No answer.

"*MOM...*"

"What?" she murmured, unfocused in her dream state.

"Did you get the Christmas letter Anne and I sent you?"

Pause. And then, just as I was about to join another conversation at the end of the table, I heard an almost inaudible, "No."

I drove by her house the next day to check on her. She was lying in bed, and I peeked in the refrigerator and under the tin foil covering the plate I made her. She hadn't eaten anything... a big "no" on the cucumber salad.

I don't care what foul thing I verbally or mentally ranted about her, the truth was I still begged for her love and recognition. I wanted her to taste that salad.

Maybe my feeling about "her time" was just me being a spook. She got up and asked for me to get her a glass of Pepsi. She always took it with a lot of ice.

By now, she was literally living on Pepsi and Pall Mall Reds.

"Mom, do you want me to take down the Christmas Tree?" I asked.

"No," she answered, not looking at me.

I don't know why I asked. She always waited or Epiphany, which was a few days off.

I stood there hoping for some kind of conversation but per usual – there was none.

"Well, I guess I should get going," I said putting on my coat.

I walked over and bent, giving my Mom a hug.

"I love you," I whispered in her ear.

I pulled away looking at her face until she met my eyes. "I love you, Mom," I said.

I think my saying this pained her – from the look in her eyes.

She passed 11 days later.

## XXXXXI.

"I am so happy for Marge," said Mrs. Hanny, a childhood friend of Mom's from way back at Immaculate Conception elementary school in the 1930s.

"She was ready to go. She'd call and tell me… ever since Derik died."

She meant well. But I wondered what it would look like if I drop kicked a 71 year-old "blue hair" on her ass in the middle of a wake.

Dad had been gone 10 years and Mom wasn't herself with no one at home with her. She missed the company… and control. In my delusional, codependent mind, I fleetingly played with the idea of actually having her come live with *Anne and me*!

The turnout at the visitation was respectable. The handkerchiefs were out; hushed conversations ensued. *Nobody knows what a dichotomy you were,* I thought looking in the casket. The left of her face was puffy and bruised a purplish-blue from where blood collected, as she laid on the heartless cold of the ceramic floor. Why couldn't they cover it up, like she did with me?

"The dear woman had all those children," I overheard.

"Not only that, but look at how well they turned out," a second replied.

I had to walk outside.

My brother, Derik, Jr. – and his wife, Janice, approached me.

"Keith," he asked, "Would you mind writing the petitions and planning the Funeral Mass with Father Martin?"

*Again,* I thought, *What is wrong with you people? You're the eldest son of eight boys; you do it! Do something other than being Dad's namesake and the carrier of a Get-Out-of-Jail FREE Card!*

"And," Janice asked, "Would you consider delivering the readings, too."

Being the people pleaser Mom made me, I agreed. Seeing me crying during one reading, people were touched at how they perceived I felt for her. I wished they could explain "how I felt" to me.

If they wanted the truth, I believe my emotions were coming alive, because she was dead.

## XXXXXII.

Shaving, I see you in the mirror. The blade skims the channels your nails have dredged. My eyes canvas scars like abstract paintings, examining shapes and sizes, what appear to be puncture wounds. These are a latent gift to remember you by. The loss of elasticity in my face makes them all the more apparent as I grow older.

I have lost most of my hair like your father and brothers. I do, as I suspected, favor your side of the family. Kenny still has his hair. His trackless complexion.

What else comes with favoring you, Mom? Will I lose all hope like my hair? Allow life's blows to stump me, turn me inward into a shut in, like you? Will my negative character traits rule me, too, to the very end? Will I live to hate like you? Or, learn to love?

## XXXXXIII.

Cleaning out her house, readying it for sale, I spied Mom's Prayer Book of Novena's on her bedside table. Curiously, I looked to see the section bookmarked. In my hand, I held the Christmas letter Anne and I sent Mom, which she claimed she had not gotten.

I still wonder if she searched for it when she got home or just couldn't remember receiving it.

It marked the Prayer for the Souls in Purgatory… souls God has deemed must pay the price for sins done on earth – in a place of limbo – suspended in time and space between heaven and hell. Only upon completing this penance will he or she someday be freed to join Him in His celestial Kingdom.

I do not believe she prayed for others; I believe she prayed for herself.

In completing the job of preparing mom's house for sale, siblings fumbled over themselves, not knowing "where to begin." This nauseated me (as they needed only to bend their backs and begin the obvious). We all knew the primary thing was for us to simply finish emptying the house and paint the interior walls. If each kid just took a room, we'd be through painting in a matter of a few hours.

Mom, over the past two years had already replaced all the windows, had a new roof put on, not to mention installed a new furnace and air-conditioning unit. Having a real-estate license in my back pocket, *This place was ready to sell.*

I went to the farthest bedroom and began by clearing out the closet of what little stuff remained, pushing it with anything else left in the room to the center of the floor, clearing the perimeter. Then, I got to work: first painting the ceiling. Checking to make sure it had dried, I masked off the edges and moved to paint the walls. The room was knocked out in a matter of an hour. This was not a big house. Having been trained well by Mom and being a naturally good painter didn't hurt. Hearing everyone find what they could to inhibit their getting started, I wanted to just tell them all to go… That I'd paint it in a day by myself (as I had done growing up). I'd never heard such pissing and moaning in my life.

I moved to the next room to knock it out. In doing so, I saw little else done around me as this had now turned into a reason to socialize. I also keenly noticed Billy and his wife finish-up loading their pick-up truck with a load of Mom's furniture. *For God's sake,* I thought, *does it never stop?* I remembered him asking just hours after Mom died, standing practically on top of the very spot – who would get the refrigerator. I was, again, infuriated. I imagined, beyond all reality, my walking outside and decking him to the ground. I shut the door and moved to paint my second room: Mom's and Dad's bedroom.

Following the same pattern of clearing out the closet first, I opened it and caught Mom's familiar scent. I immediately had a rush of memories: sneaking in here and stealing candy out of her annual Valentine's Day heart of chocolates; digging through her center dresser draw (now gone) chock full of costume jewelry that sparkled like a pirate's treasure chest; the time Mom and Dad were gone for the weekend, and I had a small party (escaping to this room to make-out with my girlfriend – only to get sick to my stomach quickly over the recognition of my being on Mom's side of the bed). The smell I now coveted. But why? This want and need in the face of all that happened between us continued to sew its sickness inside me.

I began to paint the ceiling, hearing everyone cavorting. Was everything a cause to party? *Really, I just want to get done and leave ASAP,* I thought. I heard someone claiming the industrial-gauge laundry cart Mom bought with my paycheck from working at the corner store, and my anger rose. This led me to thinking about receiving a call shortly after Dad died from one of my brothers and sisters informing me of the decision that each kid would be putting in a given amount of money toward Mom on a monthly basis to meet her needs.

I was profoundly upset by the callousness of this request in the face of Mom's and my relationship. How dare they? And what's more unbelievable is how each kid would give the same amount. So, let's see: an established lawyer and a fledgling copywriter paying in the same. If that wasn't bull crap. Anne and I were trying to make it as best we could early in our marriage and now this? She was not for it in the least. Needless to say, despite all my true assessments of the insane nature of the request and immediate desires to stand firm and say, "Absolutely not," I conceded. Again, my sonly sense of duty (my codependence, yet again) taking over. Or was I simply trying to show my siblings how self righteous I could be? Even if this was true, today I recognize they saw nothing. For their focus did not extend far beyond themselves.

After finishing this bedroom, I looked to see the third bedroom actually being worked on by two brothers (so they could talk). Even I could not look down on this. I, too, might have sought it out, but I had been long trained to work alone and silently, therefore, more quickly and efficiently. Still, due to a general lack of zeal and the gluttonous commotion of truckload after truckload being carted off, I knew I would be back the next day. But today, there was one more area I would have to tackle: the kitchen or Monster's Head, as I called it, where I was beaten all those years.

Granted, the entire room needed renovation, but – for today – the only part of this torture chamber that needed painting was the beast's scalp (or ceiling), which was yellowed severely from years of nicotine exposure, particularly in the far corner adjacent to where Mom sat. One could take a reasonable gander that her blowing it up and across the face of her friend kept a fairly constant billow of smoke circulating there.

A mere band-aid, I knew paint alone couldn't cover this. So, I left the house to buy some Kilz stain primer. I'd used it before, and it would generally take only one application to cover most anything. To my surprise, though, after painting the whole 10' x 12' ceiling with it – the yellow stain in that one particular corner eked itself through defiantly like a large swath of eczema.

I applied another coat – the biting teeth, the uneven rows of faux cobblestone at my ladder's feet – trying at each step to desperately take me down. The stain ominously reappeared and reappeared. In all, it took hours and *six coats*, each one thicker, to finally mask this heinous marking. To this day, I feel like I was working to wipe away the stain of Mom's transgressions in this room. If only momentarily. I sometimes wonder. Did it reappear, weeks… months… or even years later, to stay?

## XXXXXIV.

Shortly after, I was asked if I would take Mom's Westy Daisy. I said, "no," and I immediately felt guilty. That's what I did: felt guilty if I didn't put everyone's desires before my own. I was programmed to be at service.

I justified my refusal by considering that I already had a pet. But, since, I had come to understand I harbored resentment: *even with a dog.* The reality was I was irked with Daisy because Mom treated her better than me.

Mom would sit, after Dad died and all the kids moved out of the house, eating unhealthy and binging on sweets. Daisy shared in the éclairs and ice cream… pandered to with this treat and that. Whereas, back in the day, I was prone to be given the likes of days-old liver or stew with a roach on top.

This takes me to a summer day when I was around seven or eight and another dog. I walked by a house where I saw what I believed to be a Beagle chained to a hand rail to a door aside the driveway. I walked up to it and gave it a pet. It seemed gentle. I gave it more pets and watched its tail wag.

It is then that the sun's glint hit the shinny powered-blue body of the Chevy four-door Match Box car I held in my right hand. Without thinking, I began to roll the small car from the dog's muzzle, up its forehead, down its neck and back, ending at the tip of his tail. I remember thinking of his tail as a drawbridge.

The dog didn't seem to mind. It sat still, though I did not notice its tail ceasing to wag.

I continued driving my toy car all over the animal, when suddenly it snapped, jumping up and biting at my face. It was just one quick, sudden snap. I felt pressure against my face, and I jumped up. I was startled. I felt fine, but quickly my lip area began to hurt. I looked down and my powder blue car was getting a bright red paint job from blood dripping down my chin.

I didn't know how bad I was hurt. I began to run home. I was frightened, both by the incident and what Mom's reaction might be.

From nowhere, I could hear Kenny's voice running behind me shouting out, "One… Two… Three…"

"What… are… you… doing?" I mumbled, my hand covering my mouth, as I ran.

"Counting the blood spots!" he shouted.

Upon getting to the house, I tried to explain. I wanted Mom to be a mother, to help me.

"You stupid…"

"You what?" I recall hearing as her she slapped me around the head, me protecting my lip area by blocking her blunt hits, her smacks.

Her lips seemed to separate, revealing the gleam of yellowing enamel on sharp, serrated teeth ready once again to bite.

Only after getting her own licks in, did she take me to the doctor for stitches.

## XXXXXV.

There is no justification for harming another, especially a defenseless child. What I always called into question, but am now willing to let go, are the causes and conditions of her actions. The reasons for her displaced anger and her (and my) missing the mark. I now know my role in our other-worldly dynamic.

I am not serendipitous. Suturing up the binding of this wounded writing at the age of nearly 60, I live with PTSD and am a recovering alcoholic of nearly 15 years. Having worked the spiritual 12 Steps of Alcoholics Anonymous, I am finally able to accept. Not wishing to forget the past, nor shut the door on it. I have released the control this woman has had on me gradually over these years of sobriety, Yes, this magnificent (and maniacal) woman controlled my thoughts – even up to nearly two decades after her death.

For nearly 30 years of marriage, through good and bad, Anne has unflinchingly stood by my side (next to her: our gossamer child that might have been). She is the lead which binds me, a large part of the strength that reclaims me. I continue the slow process of soldering myself together. And thankfully, like the fractured, reclaimed pieces of a stained-glass panel, upon an unexpected and fleeting flash of light, I am more and more able to glimpse at the backlit beauty of the broken me.

## XXXXXVI.

I listen to Sarah Brightman and Andrea Bocelli sing "Time to Say Goodbye." It is my 58th birthday. I do not expect the visceral response I have as I begin to cry. *Why do I cry?* It is then that I realize it is because I am, finally, releasing myself from you. I am, too, coming to do what I never thought I could: forgive you. That is because I now understand that to forgive is not to accept the wrongs that you have done, but to stop allowing them to take my heart. This, I now recognize, is the only way for me to be reborn, to be born, really, with all the possibility of youth, even if so late in life. I know it is impossible for me to forget, though; our union will forever remain inescapable, iron-clad... This is the cross you placed on my shoulders. Still, I have and will always love you, Mom, on some level. And after 19 years since your death, with this book (which you always suspected I would write). I now say to you, simply and truly: "Goodbye."

## XXXXXVII.

*Read at Mom's and Dad's grave as part of my ninth step amends, according to the 12 Steps of Alcoholics Anonymous.*

Mom,

Looking through clear glass now, I can see *as a child* – obviously – I had no role in our dysfunction. Though admittedly, I do see my culpability in goading you in my middle teens. I used my sharp tongue and biting cynicism to retaliate against your brutality. After all, I learned from the master.

I will bury this letter here, between you and Dad, to replant myself and reclaim my rightful place among the living. Whereas, I had been told innumerable times by you, Mom, "I would never amount to anything," and other heinous remarks, this is my time to say, "No, you were wrong. And with all that is inside me, I will always love you as my Mom, yet hate you for your lack of nurturance, the utter ruination you brought to a life you were to foster. You were not my *mother*.

(And Dad, I love you too, yet hate you for not protecting me, no matter its cost in Mom's approval or appearance's sake. You were not my *father*.)

Strangely, throughout my adulthood – and although away from you, Mom, I subconsciously chose to continue the blind march of reacting to life as if living (still trapped) beneath your roof, under your control.

My belief is you lacked the proper equipment to even shoot for the mark, let alone hit it. Religion failed you; whereas, *spirituality* saved my life.

During Mass, you knew when to genuflect, kneel, and make the sign of the cross. But how to build a constant contact with God, a God consciousness which would guide your mired mental state to greener pastures – remained well beyond your understanding. For this, I feel sorry for you.

A stained-glass window depicting St. Sebastian from the exhibit at the Nelson-Atkins Museum of Art, years back, flashes before my eyes. I study it for its intended instruction. He stands victorious over his archer assassins. His right hand thrusts upward, holding the bloodied projectiles he (himself) has pulled from his upper torso: a testament to the Faithfull's promise of spiritual life over death. I take momentary pause, stitching my gaze from wound to wound – ending at his pierced heart.

Enlightened, I accept God's invitation to resuscitate my own pierced heart.

> I stand
> at the kitchen sink
> washing
> the one thing
> I took from home
> after you died:

## THE DAY THE SKY BROKE OPEN

The Madonna
and Child statue
you bought
for your mother
and regained possession of
after she passed.

It was the mother-son ideal
I meditated on,
kneeling before you,
traumatized,
loving you
year after year.

I wash it gently,
remembering
the time you unwittingly
soaked a statue of
St. Joseph – carved out of salt –
in a sink of warm water.

You did not realize
it would dissolve,
desert you
like
your man-made
religion.

Only to return
later,

*Keith T. Hoerner*

pushing your hands into the milky-white water, confused,
almost frantic,

as you thrashed
about
in search
of what you
had
laid there.

# SKY BREAK

**XXXXXVIII.**

The film shown at school goes way beyond standard fare for the discussion of *stranger danger*. It shows children on a playground approached by someone they do not know. A heavy-handed B-movie orchestra director builds to a wanton crescendo. There is the exchange of *hey-I'm-a-creepy-guy-you-shouldn't-be-talking-to* lines, the offer of candy, and the obligatory snatching. I hear blood-curdling screams off camera and see a lone girl's white Mary Jane patent-leather shoe float down a stream in the blackening woods.

Welcome to the lauded instruction of Catholic elementary schools.

The next reel is anti-abortion propaganda. I am introduced to the candy-apple baby. A fetus aborted through the use of a saline solution that burns the skin to a bright pinkish red. I am given statistics of the millions of babies killed at the hands of sinners. I am made to listen to the muffled cries of these dead-before-born martyrs piled in a literal trash can in all forms of squirming dismemberment.

Boys are separated from girls.

Father Brian stands in front of the class and tells us boys we must never touch our genitals, never masturbate. "If you do, you'll shake up the genes and have retarded children," he says. "Plus," he adds, writing the outrageously finite number of 2,749 on the board – which, honestly, seems like a really BIG number to me at the time, "this is how many ejaculations you get in a lifetime. Don't waste 'em!"

I, and the other boys, look instantly ashamed and squirm in our seats.

Walking home, we kids are instructed to seek out white stars in the windows of houses for a safe haven against the threat of stranger danger. Already traumatized by the afternoon's *curriculum*, I remember ducking behind trees at the sound of each and every car on my scamper home, scanning for stars, the security of stars. I saw a few and fantasized about rushing up to the peaceful assurances they offered: a welcome home, an inquiry of my day, a tussle of the hair as we cajoled over a snack. Though, with head hung, I knew I would have to make the trek to my real house, where the windows had no stars and where a stranger waited for me: called Mom.

This tiny, ironic anecdote is the baseline for the story of *our lives*, if you are a survivor of childhood physical, sexual, or mental abuse.

Today, at whatever age, the survivalist in us secures our refuge on a daily basis, even while that safe haven stands (door wide open) held by the likes of spouses and other loving and understanding family/friends. *They* are our *stars*, waving to us to rush forward as the boy/girl moves the man/woman to hurry in. Such is our reality, our shared truth. Because, despite their best efforts, we find ourselves traversing insidious landscapes in the shadows of each hour, both real and imagined, as a by-product of years of suffering at the misaligned willfulness of another. Our aggressor(s) either did not fully understand – or, frankly, give a damn – that we would carry the imprint of h/er hate, h/er hands on our physical selves, as well as embedded on our crippled hearts and psyches our entire lives. Recent studies have even shown that abuse such as this changes the very makeup of our DNA! *Unlike the school priest's claim against masturbation.*

What has not changed is the fact that to get a true picture of the number of children abused in America, you must only imagine hearing your phone ring *every 15 seconds.* That's right. Ring. Ring. *RING. RING. RING!* It would be frequent, unending, and unnerving to a point that the masses might finally sit up and take action.

If you are not one of *us*, this writing is as much a plea for those who suspect child abuse to take tangible steps and make the ringing stop. Too many people subscribe to social psychology's Bystander Effect and its *somebody-else-will-do-something* mantra.

As a child, I would often wonder why no one helped. The fact is: that supposed *someone else* rarely acts, and we stand – or kneel – before our abusers alone, in incomprehensible states of horror. It is a theory of inaction, and inaction breeds complacency. And complacency breeds irreparable harm and death.

I shout this and will not "dial it down" for fear there will be no answer: *because, actually, suspected child abuse is reported, not every 15, but every 9.3 seconds.*\* This is why I write.

As I walked those few miles from school, I came to know a family along the way who had kids a grade or two ahead of me, and worth noting: a star in their window. They would invite me to play, but again – head hung (my general posture) I had to tell them I couldn't for the longest time. They did not know the reason why, but one day, under one guise or another, I would be blessed to find the time to get to briefly know them and the environment in which they lived… a stable environment.

Today, teaching college students composition, I realize that even as a child, I keenly exercised the rhetorical strategy of compare and contrast. I immediately sorted the similarities (if any) and differences (many) between our lives and circumstances. I was struck by the uplifting goings-on in their home; there were crafts and activities to be done.

"Come in, Keith, if only for a few minutes, and create a plaque with us," their mother called out cheerfully.

I was introduced to the French art of decoupage, lacquering pieces of colored paper to a scrap of wood, while at the same time, forever adhering the warm spirit of their home like a healing balm to my scarred self.

*It has just come to me recently, how my resilience to live inadvertently sought out these houses, these "Star People, as I call them," who would give me the footing to survive my formative years.*

These four children and their parents freely and with abandon extended an open door to me to explore, create without care of error, take a pony ride even, until I would ask the time and startled, hurriedly unsaddle while they begged me to stay. They were like angels trumpeting the joys of heaven on earth, while I unaccustomed to such music ran home: too precocious, too young to reenact the passions of Christ.

Nearly 3 MILLION children are reported abused and neglected each year.* This is why I write.

I was struck the other day by a news story which explained how one should not attach the name of a pet to retribution: as the animal would associate, emotionally, its sheer *being* with the harshness of one's tone. This, it was purported, would damage the animal forever.

Why, I often wonder, are there so fewer child-abuse alerts? The same stands true for a child in regard to harsh words.

"Keith, you stupid, no good sissy," for example... Why could she not have dropped my name and left it at the collective *you*? Without my name attached, I could have more easily rolled her infinite, disparaging remarks over to the universe at large, rather than let them etch their way into my mind, while her tongue recoiled: catching the drool of her acidic saliva.

I watch people become rightfully enraged upon commercials for the American Association for the Care and Protection of Animals (AACPA), yet sit silent at the mere mention of child abuse.

I have been known to turn to Anne and ask, frustrated, "Why is it, people get immediately heated at the mistreatment of an animal, and turn a cold, blind eye to the abuse of a child?"

I think they see animals as helpless, unable to take care of themselves, would be the kind of answer I might hear.

Don't get me wrong. I love animals, and we have two dogs. But allow me to level the playing field. Children *are* helpless, too. CHILDREN *cannot* take care of themselves, either.

At this moment, there are also animals being given sweets (as with my mother's, perhaps yours) while a child is having h/er name (me, you, someone close) attached to a vile string of words slicing through the air undercut by a vicious blow.

Yes, to reiterate, my Mom treated the family dog better than me. So what can it be that turns adults against children and relegates them to less than animals?

Six out of 10 mothers abuse their children.* This is why I write.

I have already put forth many conjectures as to the possible cause of my Mom's abusive behavior. In researching, Maternal Narcissism keeps threading the needle, stitching together the patchwork of causations culminating in her actions. Firstly, her apparent lack of empathy kept her focused solely on her personal wants (not needs) to a fatal, psychopathic fault. Other blocks within this loosely seamed tapestry of *excuses* center around "a desire to control, as the abuser feels a lack of it in most other places of h/er *want life*," According to the U.S. Dept. of Health & Human Services. "Perpetrators perceive their lives as spinning into chaos. It is typically an anger response, and anger is often a response to fear, an extension of the flight or fight response, or a misfiring of it. Anything may be perceived as a threat. An error made by another driver... An interruption in a conversation... A dropped bowl of cereal or spilled glass of milk... An argument between siblings... An action without prior permission... A pulled shirt... A question. Whatever the spark, it is wrong and must be righted."

Substance abuse and being on the low end of the socio-economic ladder are ever-burning embers, too, stoking the fire of this maltreatment.

*In the U.S. alone, a reported 4+ children die each day due to child abuse. Also, nearly 60% of ALL child deaths are due to abuse but not reported as such.\* This is why I write.*

Having not entered kindergarten, because my mother had the legal option to negate it or not (she keeping me home to be of use to *get this or to do that*), I entered fearfully into 1st grade. I so wanted to do well, but I was already programmed to fear. I simply did not do anything right, according to Mom. So, I was sure to fail...

There was a kind of audio machine near my desk where mentally challenged kids came from a neighboring classroom and put on the headphones to conduct some sort of learning exercise. I did not know this then; I just knew that their sometimes differing appearance, movements, and vocal qualities scared me.

What scared me, really, I now understand. I feared I would slip in my lessons and be made to utilize the machine and return with these other children to their "special" classroom.

I entered school with a predetermined lack of self-worth; I was absolutely unable to muster any degree of self-confidence.

Slowly, I rooted myself, but it was difficult. Though, as mentioned, a writing teacher at the college level today, I recall sitting at home for Mom's derogatory sessions before flash cards as I simply could not learn my alphabet. It tortured me. Kenny had it down, but I would not cultivate learning for future use. I lived in the present tense for survival's sake. My Star People had not yet intervened to teach me future tense and the necessity for learning, for which memory is key.

Enter my first Star Person, Kathleen, who gently interceded and succeeded in helping me. For this and seemingly everything, she was picked out and picked on by Mom. I did not like the feeling that a bridge was being built which one day her brutal figure would cross, like the Ogre of children's fables, to gobble me up just to spit my limbs to the ground for fun and frolic. It was this adult awareness (from sufferings I witnessed Mom targeted Kathleen for) which made me grow up sooooo quickly. That and the intuitive knowledge it would – one day – be me. This was the polluted air I breathed, the stale bread I ate.

In class, I did want to be picked for one particular honor, though. Sister Martina had a special book of artwork. She encouraged us during art periods to do our very best as she would sometimes select one lucky artist to have his or her work grace the pages of a leather-bound, thick-spined tome. This is perhaps a first recollection of my competitive nature, which was another of the lifelines carrying me through my abusive childhood... for competitiveness is based in a positive sense of self. Thus, it could only have existed, at the time, apart but part me, by the grace of God. I knew in my heart I had what it took to make it in that book.

One day late in the year, we were called to take out our Crayolas and create a picture of our choice. I loved the color called Blue Green, a soothing aqua that transported me somewhere else – though I knew of no other places but the tight spaces at home and these rooms at school, where I could stare at other children and notice their new shoes and pants without patches. I especially coveted their colorful lunch boxes emblazoned with the likes of Batman and Scooby-Doo, or "cooler" yet, bands like The Monkees! My brown bag would have to do.

I *did* get one, decades later – though – from Anne as a cheerful affirmation.

Anyway, that day my artwork was complete. I looked at it closely, making finishing touches, and I was thrilled. I felt proud of it. It was on the simple side: galactic circles of different colors orbiting each other in a collection of spheres, where upon I took the eraser from my pencil and working from the center outward, blended the colors to create colorful rays of light or energy. It felt, even to a boy of eight years old, to be palpable and alive.

Sister Martina collected them and did the usual, gratuitous review.

"Mary Ellen, excellent job with shading."
"Bobbie, you sure do like your G.I. Joe; don't you."
"Betty, flowers like I've never seen..."
"Keith... Well Keith, if this isn't one of the most interesting uses of coloring I have ever seen!"

I swallowed hard, immediately associating the choice of the word "interesting" as a chide.

"Class, gather around, you must see the way..."

And her commentary carried on, resulting in the announcement that this picture would be added to her collection (if I would allow), and the request to create a duplicate picture while the others watched, so they might learn my technique and try to make one on their own.

I ran home beaming, copy in hand. I had been picked! I had made it into Sister Martina's art book!

I rushed in to show Mom, which meant Kathleen first and then Mom.

"Why so excited about a bunch of circles?" Mom asked, dropping my picture to the floor with a kind of smirk on her lips and a hint of perverse glee in her eyes.

"I don't know much about artwork, per se. (*You're a liar,* I thought. *I ALWAYS see you draw!*) Now, *work...* I *know* about, and I have some for *you*. First, get out of that school shirt."

I turned and went to my room deflated. I was picked in class for a *good,* a *positive* reason. But that was in the world out there. A world I visited, only briefly. In the world I lived in, was to always live in until middle age, I knew somehow, someway, I was being picked in a different way, for a different reason. I was a coaster to a glass of booze. An ashtray to a lit cigarette. A baseball to a bat. It would all prove true.

This unfathomable phenomenon of picking or targeting specific children for abuse is mystifying still today. To revisit our statistic that 6 out of 10 mothers abuse their children, it is also proven that women are more likely to participate in child abuse even more than men (which is difficult for society to embrace due to the simple notion that mothers are believed to be inherently drawn to nurture and support). Admittedly, this fact goes against our society's belief system. From among the long list of reasons a parent may attach the focus of abuse toward one child, I assert the following applied to my situation specifically:

Her absolute inability to bond with me as a child

Her dislike of my personality traits (e.g. effeminacy), and therefore, seeing me as flawed

My passivity (obedience reaching subservience… demanded by her but despised)

My abnormal sleep patterns (e.g. sleepwalking/bedwetting) which she could not control

Her perception of me as an adversary, the one with similar traits who might live the life she wanted, reinforcing a sense of dread, jealousy

Her unaddressed health and mental issues (Alcoholism and Maternal Narcissism, et al)

A parent who targets a specific child for abuse has a hazy sense as to who the child is and represents, taking out h/er frustrations misguidedly. The circumstances of h/er very being, esoteric as it may seem, sets target children up for continual thrusts of unjustifiable, malicious torture.

*The selection of children to abuse does not discriminate; it crosses genders, as well as all socio-economic and racial lines.\* This is why I write.*

I had my first drink in seventh grade having just relocated to the neighborhood after our one-and-only move. I was with a group of kids, socially uncomfortable and wanting to make friends, something Kenny had already done. These were them; I was just along as an allowance to Kenny. He… cool. Me… not. Still, I was bolstered by his presence as usual. He always took a protective air about me.

I remember finding ourselves along a set of railroad tracks by the high school. Beer made its appearance. I was encouraged to drink. I don't remember seeing Kenny drink, but I generally waited for his cue to do anything. I did not like it. It tasted bad. Still, as I sipped on it over an hour (afraid to be ridiculed or to embarrass Kenny), I began to feel my first buzz. I may have not liked the taste, but the false courage and lack of caring it gave me, presented an escape I longed for every waking moment. *Mom and everything about her just vaporized from my mind.* I would, soon enough, find myself seeking this escape in an ever-escalating manner, though I did not identify it at the time. I was, after all, just a kid.

And escalate it did. A couple years later, I would find myself standing outside liquor stores asking older strangers to grab me a six-pack of beer or a cheap bottle of booze like Mad Dog 20/20, paving a path to me skimming the liquor cabinets of classmates' parents. It didn't take but a few more years for me to tap the source directly by way of my first job as a stock boy at, you guessed it, the corner liquor store! My search for that feeling of "normalcy" which eluded me was now to be found in my newest and truest "friend."

He stood watch, his dark and shifty shadow beside me as I dropped my stash in with the trash and took it out… only to retrieve it later after work. Head first in a dumpster, legs flailing in search of my reprieve. I knew it was wrong; I knew no other way.

At the age of 44, I would find *that other way* but not before collecting multiple DWIs and proving myself a threat to myself and the community, sure to also prove deadly without intervention. Too, I would identify my perceived best friend as a foe.

As part of my on-going recovery, I now reach out to help abuse victims now fighting for recovery from addiction – as others reached out their hands to me.

He is pumped with adrenaline, as fidgety as a five-year old; we sit in a sandwich shop, me buying his lunch, as he and his wife are strapped for cash, hold up with a friend for weeks. Waiting for a small military pension to arrive the coming Monday after Easter, he has already filed an application – as I encouraged – at an apartment complex in the hope of establishing their own residence as quickly as possible. A step toward regaining a footing…

This stay with a friend is propagated by a relapse on Michael's part into alcohol- and crack-cocaine use: leading to the loss of his job, his wife, estrangement from his three children. and a marriage to this second wife after only twenty-something days of meeting her. They have two months of marriage behind them and don't seem to get along. After all, they are just now getting to know each other and question their compatibility.

These are the types of entanglements that happen in the fog of addiction.

Michael says he isn't hungry, but with encouragement, he orders something substantial *and gobbles it down*. Then, he hits me for a loan to be paid back after the coming Easter weekend. I say, "No."

Though I have the hundred bucks, this would enable him and his behavior, and Mike is too use to manipulating those around him to take on the burden of his actions. Unless Michael stops this, and a number of other behaviors, he is sure to be lost. Sadly, even now, he and his wife are just a few friends and a roll of quarters away from being on the street.

*This* is what makes me sad.

"Remember what you told me the other day," I ask. "That you could find your way, manipulate your way to getting any drug you wanted… That you don't have to worry about where your next meal is coming from?"

He stares at me. He searches for my soft spots, and I admittedly fight my innate inclination to hand over the money. But, I do not. My recovery program has enabled me to control my co-dependent nature, the taking on of other's problems as my own. "Work this out. Learn to settle the unmanageability you create in your life," I say. "Only then will you be on a lasting path to sobriety."

"How long have you been clean?" I ask.

"Twenty eight days. It'll be... thirty... thirty days on Sunday," he says.

We celebrate the first month of sobriety in recovery circles.

"Do you see the metaphor in that?" I ask, thinking of his thirty-day mark falling on Easter Sunday: the day of Christ's resurrection into exalted life.

"I don't know," he says, looking distracted. A spiritual man, Michael catches me a little off guard with his answer. I can see in his eyes the surprise, the defeat of his inability to eek money out of me.

I can sense he has made assurances to his wife that I'd be an easy roll. But, I have become stronger. And he knows I am right not to.

This is what makes this particular Good-Friday feel so bad.

About two-thirds of those in substance abuse programs have experienced some kind of child abuse.* This is why I write.

The concussions football players receive and the long-term health effects of these injuries is, presently, a hot topic of debate. Though hardly a player of sports, I live not only with the same physical manifestations of having had my brain beat loose, but the additional compounding of emotional concussions ad infinitum (without the benefit of outlandish pay). This ingrained, walking-on-eggshells scrimmage through life, led to an insatiable will to survive given my unconscious brushes with Star People and my childish but fervent faith in God. This is, perhaps, the one thing I can thank my parents for: *sending me to a parochial school.* Like a moth to flame, I was later able to escape the darkness to a newfound spiritual relationship with my Higher Power that always lit the way, re-establishing a platform for redirecting my descent downward.

Trending, too, is that child-free-by-choice lifestyles are acceptable, whereby when my Mom and Dad got married, it was a cultural stigma. Still, I think my Mom (more so than Dad) should have heeded her inner desires or been born to marry in more current times. As evidenced by this story, she did not have the fortitude to parent. Her attempt was nothing more than a constant acting out against a system she felt trapped and imprisoned in. Her lashings out may have been her own cries for help, a fighting or pushing back of her inner child (singled out for some of her own picking on by a gang of social dictates on the playground of the '50s).

The irony is psychologists have shown little scientific data to prove the existence of any maternal instinct to want to have children or to support that women are natural caregivers. However, the instinct to nurture is considered to be based in genetics. This makes me wish I had the resources to have known the deepest wishes/genetic dispositions regarding motherhood in my parents' lineage, but alas I do not.

What I do know is Mom was not cut from the cloth meant to swaddle infants… and this cloth bound my wrists, causing me to struggle through even the simplest tasks of life until midway (and even still if gone unchecked). I rolled recklessly like a pinball here and there, causing virtually everyone to put up h/er bumper barricades for fear of being hit by another of my poor aims at relationships… inconsistent, reckless behaviors fueled by an ever-increasing use of alcohol and own, self-absorbed narcissistic behavior. After all, she was my role model in this regard.

Today, I continue to work a daily balance toward life: putting God first, others second, and myself third. This principle is at the heart of AA practices, which are based on the teachings of The Bible. *I encourage you to seek out the support groups/professional counseling you need.* This is why I write.

How resilient are you? The hot button in psychology today, pertaining to abused children, has to do with this notion of resiliency. For me, I found myself to be more resilient than perhaps I knew. Yes, I had a way to scrape by, put forth more than a stiff upper lip, to live (not necessarily thrive) through years of abject torment. Still, why did I have the resiliency to not kill myself, when so many others take this route?

If you are reading this, *you, too,* have proved more resilient than you might have thought. As Hemingway puts forth in *A Farewell to Arms,* "The world breaks everyone. And afterward some are strong in the broken places."

The key sign to this strength, studies in resiliency show, is the ability to "recruit" surrogate caregivers and adult mentors (my Star People)... often times a sibling (Kathleen, who raised me until leaving home), a coach or teacher (Sisters Martina and Barbara in the first and third grades, respectively), the family on the way to elementary school who did what they could to nurture me, other friends and their families (a high-school buddy, Jerry, and his parents, Shannon and Eppy), support groups like AA (thank you – Lynnette), and – of course – Anne...

Resiliency for me was the ability to take their vicarious support and love, and cocoon myself, creating an impenetrable chrysalis through which Mom could not tear. Through this self preservation, I could — *as you could* — sustain a suspended frame of mind and body, which God would (in His time) morph into full-flighted fruition: our clear, skeletal bodies now unweighted and brilliant.

Notice the necessity for God in this equation (at least, for me).

The enlightenment of spirituality proved the side stiles to the ladder of my recovery. And, it is sure to do so for you, if embraced. This spirituality was the willingness for me to open my mind to the unquestioning truth that there is a Higher Power, beyond myself, who has always been pointing the way toward my intended path.

The celebrated psychologist Carl Jung advocated the necessity of a spiritual component for anyone wishing to find relief from the causes and conditions of alcoholism. He deemed it out of the hands of mortals. Personally, I would also have to extend this theory to any illness.

This was a difficult reality I would have to work on: smashing my ego to realize that my will would have to be replaced by His will.

Still, with all my inner kicking and screaming, His will *was* being made known to me: even if unrecognizable most of the time. I heeded this message clearly one day at mass,

"And he said unto me, Write: for these words are true and faithful. And he said unto me, It is done. I am Alpha and Omega, the beginning and the end. I will give unto him that is athirst of the fountain of the water of life freely. He that overcometh shall inherit all things; and I will be his God, and he shall be my son."

— Revelation 21 The Holy Bible (KJV)

Suddenly, upon the speaking of these very words, the incessant rain deluging my soul ceased. I could hear the sky break open (the release and woosh of thousands of arrows cracking the centuries old stained-glass windows into sheets and shards of clouded rubble). The sun demanded its entree—resting at the feet of the tabernacle and surrounding my being. I felt God's paternal touch on me. In that moment, I realized that while my earthly parents failed me, my heavenly father claimed me as His son and waited to fill my emotional and psychological voids.

Resentments are events/feelings continually relived again, and again, and again. *You can stop this through a personal relationship with your Higher Power.* This is why I write.

For years, I tried to write about this but could not. Finally, I could (having become stronger in the broken places). Writing and healing are undeniably linked, The University of Texas' Dr. James Pennebaker writes in his text *Opening Up: The Healing Power of Expressing Emotions*. "Suppressed thoughts, emotions, and actions result in illness. More than purging, writing about trauma affects mental and immune functions… reducing anxiety and depression… with over 70% of those studied reporting that writing helped them to understand both the event(s) and themselves better."

*I* found this to be true. And this truth did set me on the path to freedom. I recommend *you* give it a try. Take a defining moment in your life, and (at first) write about it in 150 words or less. Note: it may help to revisit one or two of the earlier, briefer chapters herein.

Remember that writing:
Brings out what is trapped within you, lessening its larger-than-life, debilitating nature (while breaking down your abusive past – or present – into smaller, more-manageable pieces, making them easier to process and ultimately to reconcile).

Frees up feelings... you will begin to close the chapter(s) on your abuse with each healing line of narration, each healing verse. This is why I write.

*Take from these pages what helps you: not only to survive but to prosper!*

And to think, *I* initially said "*no*" upon every encouragement to write this self story. I am blessed to have finally done so... for I discovered the power of words to transform wounds. You see, one day, I did not say "no" but did the best I could and *wrote about* "*no*," leading to this ending poem and the beginnings of this book:

"I do not want to go there."
"It will help you," Anne says. "It will help others."
I do not want to root there.
The cellar is deep, and dark, and dank.
"It is not a place I can easily return from," I say.
"It terrifies me. I am so very terrified."
She persists; I acquiesce. I dig deep and let it bury me, dragmein
Out of spring's redemption.
Back to winter's bone,
Back to winter's cave of cold.
Lord, is it coincidence today is Good Friday?
On this day of all things crucified,
I am, again, given the promise of resurrection,
When tombs' rock closures
*roll* o p e n.

*U.S. Department of Health and Human Services.

Your Self Story in 150 Words or Less:

_____

_____

_____

_____

_____

_____

_____

_____

_____

_____

_____

_____

_____

_____

*Keith T. Hoerner*

## THE DAY THE SKY BROKE OPEN

*Keith T. Hoerner*

**Questions for Book Clubs:**

1) How could you individually or as a member of society assist victims of child abuse in a more effective manner?
2) Who were the Star People in your life (even if you were not a victim of abuse)?
3) How can you work to serve as a Star Person to those around YOU?
4) What are your feelings about target children, recovery programs, a Higher Power, a narcissist parent, the lasting effects of child abuse, or (insert your own topic)?

To get help for yourself or someone you love, contact:

The National Child Abuse Hotline: 1-800-4-A-CHILD (1-800-422-4453)

Adult Children of Alcoholics: www.adultchildren.org

Alcoholics Anonymous: www.aa.org

# *Epilogue*

I see my brother Jeff: a relative stranger to my upbringing, my life, furiously wrapping books in colorful, three-dimensional "shippers" that look playful like a house. Curiously, I look closer and see it is this book, my book, and a rush of love comes over me as I feel his support. He is at my back.

There is such industry: packages sprawled across the floor. I wonder… how has he solicited so many orders? Then, through the blur of this activity, I see the book has a new cover, the sheen of silver; still, I do not care. I am in the embrace of a sibling's understanding, not another reproach for telling *the secret*.

His wife, Katlyn, appears.

"How did you…" I mutter.

"There's *money* to be made," he says, looking up at me with a ravenous smile from his heap of to-be-shipped and to-be-packaged parcels.

"But… any money… is supposed… to benefit charity," I mutter.

*What is wrong with me? Why is my voice so swallowed, inaudible?* I think.

I pick-up one of the books when Katlyn says, "It needed the scene with *the cage* to really bring it together."

Somehow, I feel they *absorb the gravity*, the core of my story, and the purpose behind telling it. She is a school teacher; so I do not flinch at the remark or the thought of a revision. Still, a sense of oddness strikes me… that Jeff and Katlyn are busying themselves with this – on the back end of my book's release. More so, that I had no idea…

I open the book and my eyes vibrate as if stuck on a playful, hyper-colored picture of a young boy walking through an airport, a large caged structure of soaring beams. He marvels at the crowd; he points outside a window at a wondrous flurry of snow and the wide-winged warriors he will soon board. *It is idyllic, and it feels disingenuous.* This is *not* me. This is *not* my experience.

My countenance changes. My vocal chords rush with blood as I begin to shout out, "NO! What have you done? What are you doing? *This is not my story!*"

A blur of an exchange ensues. My voice has a melancholic scrape of pain. There is a plea to stop changing my fact into fiction. Only for me to drop the book on the floor at my feet, to have the light of the room move over me like a cloud changing the book's cover from a searing silver to a barely comprehensible, holographic picture of fucking *Santa Clause.*

My mind fights to reach the surface. It finds breath from this night fright… This awful awareness that even after telling it, there will surely be those who do not wish to accept my reality, but rather, another, shinier retelling.

# Trends in Child Maltreatment
## by ChildTrends.org

While legal definitions of child maltreatment vary by state, four types are generally recognized: physical abuse, sexual abuse, neglect (including educational neglect, medical neglect, and other forms), and emotional maltreatment. In the national statistical system that tracks child maltreatment, children are counted as victims if an investigation by a state child welfare agency classifies their case as either "substantiated" or "indicated" child maltreatment. Substantiated cases are those in which an allegation of maltreatment or risk of maltreatment was supported or founded according to state law or policy. Indicated cases are those in which an allegation of maltreatment or risk of maltreatment could not be substantiated, but there was reason to suspect maltreatment or the risk of maltreatment.[1]

From 1990 to 1994, the number of cases of child abuse or neglect that were either substantiated or indicated[2] rose from 861,000 to 1,032,000, reaching a rate of 15 per 1,000 children under age 18 in 1994. From 1994 to 1999, the trend reversed, with the number of cases dropping to 829,000, a rate of 12 per thousand, in 1999. The number of cases increased slightly from 1999 to 2001; then it leveled off until 2006, with the rate staying fairly constant throughout that period. After a sharp drop in both rate and number of maltreated children (excluding duplicate cases) from 2006 to 2007, the number and rate of maltreated children continued to decline until 2012, when both began to rise again. In 2017, there were approximately 674,000 maltreated children substantiated in the United States, a rate of 9 per thousand. Note that these data reflect states' definitions of what constitutes maltreatment; these definitions vary across states and may change over time (Appendix 1).

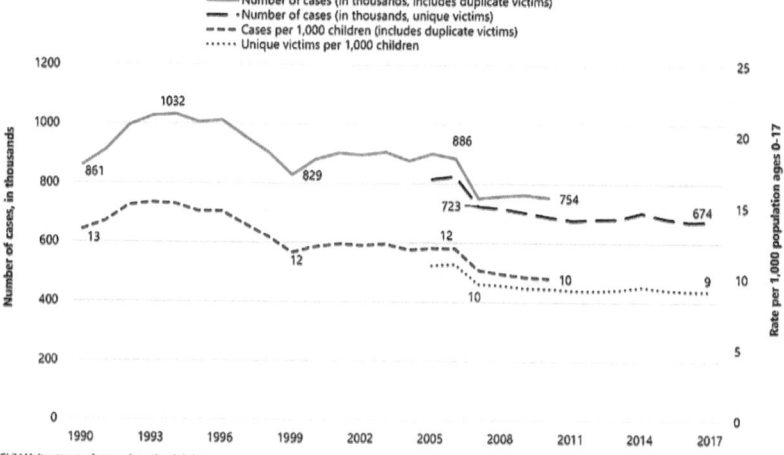

Number and Rate of Child Maltreatment* Cases/Victims: 1990-2017

**Differences by age**

Young children experience higher rates of maltreatment than older children. In 2017, children 3 and younger had a maltreatment rate of 15 per 1000, compared with 10 per 1000 for children ages 4 to 7, 8 per 1000 for ages 8 to 11, 7 per 1000 for ages 12 to 15, and 5 per 1000 for children ages 16 to 17 (Appendix 2).

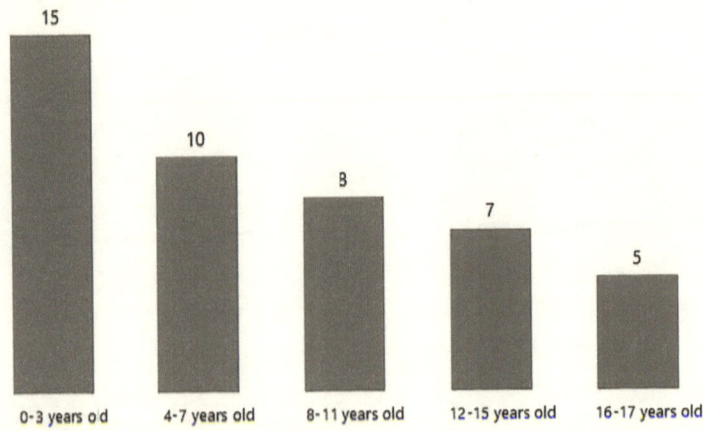

Young children experience higher rates of maltreatment than older children. In 2017, children 3 and younger had a maltreatment rate of 15 per 1000, compared with 10 per 1000 for children ages 4 to 7, 8 per 1000 for ages 8 to 11, 7 per 1000 for ages 12 to 15, and 5 per 1000 for children ages 16 to 17 (Appendix 2).

## Differences by race and Hispanic origin[2]*

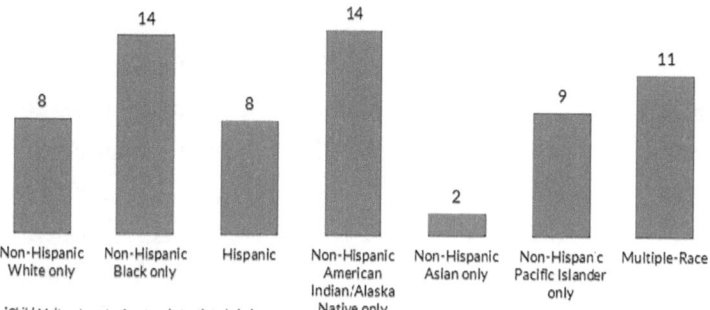

Child Maltreatment* Rate (Unique Victims per 1,000 Population), by Race[1] and Hispanic Origin: 2017

*Child Maltreatment refers to substantiated victims
[1] Estimates for specific race groups have been revised to reflect the new OMB race definitions, and include only those who are identified with a single race. Hispanics may be of any race.
Source: U.S. Department of Health & Human Services, Administration for Children and Families, Administration on Children, Youth, and Families, Children's Bureau. (2019). Child Maltreatment 2017. Retrieved from https://www.acf.hhs.gov/cb/research-data-technology/statistics-research/child-maltreatment

childtrends.org

Reflecting numerous factors, including poverty and institutional biases, non-Hispanic black, American Indian or Alaska Native, and multiple-race children have higher rates of reported child maltreatment than other children. In 2017, the reported maltreatment rate for non-Hispanic black children was 14 per 1,000 children, 14 per 1,000 for American Indian and Alaska Native children, and 11 per 1,000 for multiple-race children. This compares with rates of 9 for non-Hispanic Pacific Islander children, 8 for Hispanic children, 8 for non-Hispanic white children, and 2 for non-Hispanic Asian children (Appendix 2).

[2] Estimates for white, black, American Indian/Alaskan Native and Asian/Pacific Islander youth in this report do not include Hispanic youth. Hispanic children and youth may be of any race.

## Differences by type of maltreatment

Rates of reported neglect are higher than those for other types of child maltreatment. In 2017, 7 children per 1,000 were reported victims of neglect, compared with 2 for physical abuse, 1 for sexual abuse, and 1 for psychological or emotional abuse (Appendix 2).

Among all reported maltreated children, the proportion with reported neglect increased from 49 percent in 1990 to 75 percent in 2017, while those with reported sexual abuse declined from 17 to 9 percent, and the share with reported physical abuse declined from 27 to 18 percent. Less frequent types of maltreatment, including those classed as "unknown," accounted for the balance (Appendix 1).

Rates of physical and sexual abuse have declined over the past two decades, while rates of neglect have fluctuated and remained the highest among the types of maltreatment. From 1990 to 2017, rates of substantiated physical abuse declined by 40 percent and sexual abuse rates by 62 percent; by contrast, rates of substantiated neglect fell by 8 percent over this period.[3]

## Other estimates

### State and local estimates

State estimates for 2017 are available at U.S. Department of Health and Human Services, Administration for Children and Families, Administration on Children, Youth, and Families, Youth and Families, Children's Bureau. (2019). *Child maltreatment 2017* [Tables 3.1-3.8]. Washington, DC: Author. Retrieved from https://www.acf.hhs.gov/sites/default/files/cb/cm2016.pdf.

The KIDS COUNT Data Center also has state-level data, including the percent of victims who received post-investigation services, available at: KIDS COUNT Data Center. (2019). National kids count [Data tool]. Baltimore, MD: Annie E Casey Foundation. Retrieved from https://datacenter.kidscount.org/data#USA/2/35/36,37,38,41,40/char/0.

**International estimates**

Estimates of child maltreatment in European countries are available from the World Health Organization: World Health Organization. (2013). Scale and consequences of the problem. In D. Sethi, M. Bellis, K. Hughes, R. Gilbert, F. Mitis, & G. Galea (Eds.), *European report on preventing child maltreatment*. Geneva, Switzerland: Author. Retrieved from http://www.euro.who.int/en/health-topics/disease-prevention/violence-and-injuries/publications/2013/european-report-on-preventing-child-maltreatment.

**Data and appendices**

**Data sources**

- Data for 2000-2017: U.S. Department of Health and Human Services, Administration for Children and Families, Children's Bureau. (2002-2019). *Child maltreatment 2000-2017*. Washington, DC: Author. Retrieved from https://www.acf.hhs.gov/cb/research-data-technology/statistics-research/child-maltreatment.
- Additional data for 2000-2001:S. Department of Health and Human Services, Centers for Disease Control and

Prevention, National Center for Health Statistics. (2003). *2000 and 2001 Population Estimates for Calculating Vital Rates*. Washington, DC: Author. Retrieved from http://www.cdc.gov/nchs/about/major/dvs/popbridge/popbridge.htm.

- Data for 1990-1999 (except rate per thousand): U.S. Department of Health and Human Services, Office of the Assistant Secretary for Planning and Evaluation. (2001). *Trends in the well-being of America's children and youth 2001* [Table HC 2.10]. Washington, DC: Author. Retrieved from https://aspe.hhs.gov/report/trends-well-being-americas-children-and-youth-2001.

- Data on rate per thousand for 1990-1999: U.S. Department of Health and Human Services, Administration for Children and Families, Children's Bureau. (2000). *Child maltreatment 1999*. Washington, DC: Author. Retrieved from http://www.acf.hhs.gov/programs/cb/pubs/cm99/index.htm.

**Raw data source**

U.S. Department of Health and Human Services, Children's Bureau, National Child Abuse and Neglect Data System (NCANDS). http://www.acf.hhs.gov/programs/cb/resource/about-ncands

**Appendices**

Appendix 1. Number of Cases/Victims of Child Maltreatment, Rate per Thousand Population, and Percent Distribution by Various Characteristics: 1990-2017

Appendix 2. Child Maltreatment Cases/Victims, Rates per Thousand Population Ages 0-17, by Selected Characteristics: 2000-2017

## Background

### Definition

Child maltreatment can be defined as "behavior towards [a child] . . . which (a) is outside the norms of conduct, and (b) entails a substantial risk of causing physical or emotional harm. Behaviors included will consist of actions and omissions, ones that are intentional and ones that are unintentional."[4] Four types of maltreatment are generally recognized, including physical abuse, sexual abuse, neglect (including educational neglect, medical neglect, and other forms), and emotional maltreatment. Before 2009, all data in this report represent all substantiated or indicated cases from reporting states in a given year. For 2009 and subsequent years, duplicate victims (that is, those reported to have experienced more than one incidence of maltreatment) are excluded, and data represent the number of children who had at least one substantiated or indicated case in that year. Not all states report duplicate victims, so the total number of unique victims is an estimate based on available numbers. Legal definitions of maltreatment vary by state.

### Citation

*Child Trends. (2019). Child maltreatment. Retrieved from https://www.childtrends.org/indicators/child-maltreatment.*

### Endnotes

[1] States use different terminology to refer to the status of maltreatment reports that have, upon investigation, yielded evidence that abuse or neglect has occurred.

[2] U.S. Department of Health and Human Services, Administration for Children and Families, Children's Bureau. (2012). *Child maltreatment 2011*. Washington, DC: Author. Retrieved from http://www.acf.hhs.gov/programs/cb/resource/child-maltreatment-2011.

[3] Finkelhor, D., Saito, K., & Jones, L. M. (2016). *Updated trends in child treatment*. Durham, NH: University of New Hampshire, Crimes Against Children Research Center. Retrieved from http://www.unh.edu/ccrc/pdf/Updated%20trends%202014.pdf.

[4] Christoffel, K. K., Scheidt, P. C., Agran, P. F., Kraus, J. F., McLoughlin, E., & Paulson, J. A. (1992). Standard definitions for childhood injury research: Excerpts of a conference report. *Pediatrics, 89*(6), 1027-1034.

# *About the Author*

**Keith T. Hoerner** (BS, MFA) lives, teaches, and pushes words around in Southern Illinois. He is the founding editor of *The Dribble Drabble Review* and has been the featured in numerous national / international literary journals, anthologies, and other publications. This is his first book.

www.ingramcontent.com/pod-product-compliance
Lightning Source LLC
Chambersburg PA
CBHW021446070526
44577CB00002B/278